Human Rights in International Criminal Law

Article 53 Should Be The Voice Of Victims Under The Rome Statute Of ICC

Human Rights in International Criminal Law

Article 53 Should Be The Voice Of Victims Under The Rome Statute Of ICC

Denakpon Luc Rodrigue Tchobo

ELIVA PRESS

ISBN: 978-99949-8-027-7

Cover Design: Eliva Press
Cover Image: Freepik Premium
Email: info@elivapress.com
Website: www.elivapress.com

This Eliva Press imprint is published by the registered company Eliva Press Global Ltd. part of Eliva Press S.R.L. Publishing Group

The registered company address is: Pope Hennessy Street Level 2, Hennessy Tower Port Louis, Mauritius
Eliva Press S.R.L. Publishing Group address is: Bulevardul Moscova 21, Chisinau, Moldova, Europe

HUMAN RIGHTS IN INTERNATIONAL CRIMINAL LAW: ARTICLE 53 SHOULD BE THE VOICE OF VICTIMS UNDER THE ROME STATUTE OF ICC.

by

DENAKPON LUC RODRIGUE TCHOBO

Doctor of Juridical Science

School of Law

CASE WESTERN RESERVE UNIVERSITY

Dissertation Committee

Professor Michael J. Benza (Primary Faculty Advisor and Committee Member)

Professor Jonathan Gordon (SJD Program Director and Committee Member)

Professor and Dean Michael P. Scharf (Second Faculty Advisor and Chair of the Committee)

Contents

TABLE OF CASES

Table Of Treaties

Human Rights

International Humanitarian Law

Protocol Additional to the Geneva Conventions of 12 August 1949, and relating to the Protection of Victims of International Armed Conflicts (AP I), adopted 8 June 1977 131, 182

Protocol Additional to the Geneva Conventions of 12 August 1949 and relating to the Protection of Victims of Non-International Armed Conflicts (AP II), adopted 8 June 1977 147

Convention on the Non-Applicability of Statutory Limitations to War Crimes and Crimes Against Humanity, adopted on Nov. 26 (1968) 56

Geneva Protocol for the Prohibition of the Use in War of Asphyxiating, Poisonous or Other Gases of Bacteriological Methods of Warfare, Doc. C. 362 M. 135 1927 IX (1927) 81

International criminal law

Rome Statute of the International Criminal Court, adopted 17 July 1998, by the United Nations Diplomatic Conference of Plenipotentiaries on the Establishment of an International Criminal Court, A/CONF.183/9

General international law

U.N. Charter 165

Vienna Convention on the Law of Treaties, adopted 23 May 1969, UNTS vol. 1155, A/CONF.39/11/Add.2 236

G.A. Res. 3314, 29 U.N. G.A.O.R. Supp. (No. 31) at 142, U.N. Doc. A/9631 (1974) 80

Convention on the Prohibition of the Development Production and Stockpiling of Bacteriological (Biological) and Toxic Weapons and on their Destruction, 27 U.N. G.A.O.R. Supp. (No. 30) at 17, U.N. Doc. A/8189 (1970) 85

Treaty Banning Nuclear Weapon Tests in the Atmosphere, in Outer Space and Under Water, Aug. 5, 1963, 14 U.S.T. 1313, T.I.A.S. No. 5433 81

Treaty on the Prohibition of The Emplacement of Nuclear Weapons on the Sea Bed and The Ocean Floor and in the Sub-Soil Thereof, 25 U.N. G.A.O.R. Supp. (No. 28) at 11, U.N. Doc. A/8189 (1970) 81

Treaty on Principles Governing the Activities of States in Exploration and Use of Outer Space, Including the Moon and Other Celestial Bodies, Jan. 27, 1967, 18 U.S.T. 2410, T.I.A.S. No. 6347; Antarctic Treaty, Dec. 1, 1959, 12 U.S.T. 794, T.I, S. No. 4780 81

G.A. Res. 2840 (XXVI), P 4, U.N. Doc A/8429 Dec.18, (1971) 122

G.A. Res. 3074 (XXVIII), P 1, U.N. Doc A/9030 Dec. 3, (1973) 123

UN Declaration of Basic Principles of Justice for Victims of Crime and Abuse of Power, adopted by UN General Assembly Resolution 40/34 of 29 November 1985 124

ACKNOWLEDGEMENT

I especially thank my faculty advisor, Ms. Elizabeth H. Woyczynski, without whom this would have been be a failure. She demonstrated within her academic duty her devotion to advise and support me during tough times from my LL.M program to Doctorate degree. She emotionally supports me like my mom. Thank you Liz! I also especially thank my criminal law professor and doctorate supervisor, Michael J. Benza, for his unimaginable and amazing support. He made me challenge myself intellectually from the beginning of this project up to its end. He built my intellectual capacity to be ready for the academic community.

I am grateful for Mr. Andrew (Andy) Dorchak for his library support in the realization of this project. He is always available any time to provide me his unimaginable assistance. Very nice and humble person. Thanks for your materials support Andy. I also extremely thank Samara Benza who made this paper look linguistically professional. Once again, thank you so much Samara for your insightful support.

I additionally thank Professor Jonathan Gordon, and Professor Lewis Katz for their amazing and insightful guidance in the research and preparation of this thesis; Dean Michael P. Scharf, and Associate Dean Avidan Cover for their intrinsic support.

I am extremely grateful for my sisters Lilas Tchobo and Jasmine Tchobo, my little brother Reilinght Tchobo, and friends, as well to my lovely mom who never stopped supporting me in my journey to success.

ABBREVIATIONS AND ACRONYMS

ABBREVIATIONS

ACHPR African Commission on Human and Peoples' Rights

ACHR American Convention on Human Rights

ECCC Extraordinary Chambers in the Courts of Cambodia

GA United Nations General Assembly

GC Geneva Convention

IACHR Inter-American Commission on Human Rights

IACtHR Inter-American Court of Human Rights

ICC International Criminal Court

ICCPR International Covenant on Civil and Political Rights

ICCSt Rome Statute of International Criminal Court

ICJ International Court of Justice

ICRC International Committee of the Red Cross

ICTR Ad hoc Tribunal for Rwanda

ICTY Ad hoc Tribunal for Former Yugoslavia

ILC International Law Commission

OHCHR United Nations Office of the High Commissioner for Human Rights

UDHR Universal Declaration of Human Rights

UNHCR United Nations High Commissioner for Refugees

Acronyms

FE Factual Element

IP Investigation and Prosecution

KF Key Factors

LE Legal Element

LEFE Legal Element and Factual Element

NC Nature of Crime

ABSTRACT

Although the International Criminal Court was created to put an end to the gravest human rights abuses, its objective is sometimes challenged, in detriment to victims, because of the ambiguity that the phrase "interests of justice" in Article 53 raises. This thesis aims to examine the legal spirit of those provisions in order to protect human dignity. It attempts to lift the ambiguity that rises from those articles, and further exposes the gaps of core crimes of this statute which substantially affect the protection of human rights. This thesis concludes that the investigation and prosecution of international crimes pursuant to Article 5 of the Rome Statute are crucial under the provisions of Article 53. Thus, it suggests a doctrinal approach resulting in a formula for "the interests of justice." It proposes further the adoption of a draft called Convention for the Prevention and Punishment of "Groupicide" that aims at refining the genocide Convention.

Part I: Theoretical Background

Chapter 0: Introduction

I-Motivation

"I can't breathe! I can't breathe! I can't breathe!". With those words African American George Floyd sadly left our society with an eternal, definitive and irrevocable silence. Today Derek Chauvin, the Minneapolis police officer, has been found guilty on all charges in George Floyd's death. Meanwhile, society attempts to negotiate peace with those who killed thousands of millions of people in order to shield them from impunity. Particularly in Uganda thousands of million human beings were killed, girls and women were raped, boys and men were tortured, and were kids abducted and, transformed in child soldiers by Joseph Kony, the *so-called* "Lord of Resistance Army," and his members. However, about two decades ago, the ICC's Office of the Prosecutor suggested to suspend the investigation in Uganda situation because of existing and ongoing political peace processes. The Office of the Prosecutor stated that he would invoke the concept of "the interests of justice" to justify that suspension. Can peace exist without justice?

When Derek Chauvin's trial verdict came out, I saw and read the real meaning of justice. Indeed, the reaction, the emotion, the relief, the satisfaction feeling expressed by George Floyd's family, by our nation the United States of America, and by the world depicts peace for justice.

My role as lawyer is not to defend the crime, but rather defend people and promote justice. "The problems we face today...are human-created problems which can be resolved through human effort, understanding and the development of a sense of brotherhood and sisterhood. We need to cultivate a universal responsibility for one another and the planet we share. "[1]

The serious violations of international human rights law and of international humanitarian law constitute a crime with regard to international law. All States party to the UN Charter "have the duty to investigate" and "whether there is evidence," they ought to prosecute and punish the alleged perpetrators for accountability. However, "in these cases, States should, in accordance with international law, cooperate with one another" in order to "assist international judicial organs competent in the investigation and prosecution of these violations."[2]

Since the International Criminal Court was created in order to put an end to the gravest human rights abuses of concern in the international community,[3] the use of Article 53 of its statute (the Rome Statute) still raises ambiguity controverting its object. Many scholars have attempted to solve this problem by illuminating the concept of " the interests of justice" in order to enforce the system of international criminal justice.[4] But, there is unfortunately a huge divergence of views

---

[1] The Dalai Lama.

[2] *See* Van Boven/ Bassiouni Principles,<< Basic Principles and Guidelines on the Right to a Remedy and reparation for Victims of Gross violations of International Human Rights Law and serious violations of International humanitarian law>>, adopted by the Commission on Human Rights in its resolution 2005/35 of 19 April 2005 and by the Economic and Social Council in its resolution 2005/30 of 25 July 2005, in which the Council recommended to the UN General Assembly that also adopted it and proclaimed in its resolution 60/147 of 16 December 2005. Available at https://www.ohchr.org. (Accessed on Apr.7, 2020). This principle emphasizes that there is a "duty" to investigate and, without any qualification other than sufficiency of the evidence, to prosecute.

[3] *See* Paras. 4 and 5 of the Rome Statute (ICCSt.) Preamble.

[4] Michael Scharf, "*The Amnesty exception to the Jurisdiction of the International Criminal Court*," Cornell International Law Journal, vol. 32 (1999), 507, 521-22. ; also *see* Mahnoush H. Arsanjani, "*The Rome Statute of the International Criminal Court*," American Journal of International Law, vol. 22 (1999), p.38; Giuliano Turone,

on the legal interpretation of provisions of this article.[5] Among those scholars we have Van Boven, Michael P. Scharf, Diane Orentlicher, Talita De-Souza Dias, Elisabeth B. Ludwin King, Kate Allan, Kristin Henrard, Giuliano Turone, and C. Gallavin. Indeed, Van Boven thinks that the protection of victims is crucial by adopting the principle of Bassiouni (Van Bovin/Bassioni, 2005). In this regard, (Michael P. Scharf, 1999) supporting (Diane, 1991) asserts that obligation to extradite is the alternative international obligation of State concern. Although Michael promotes the prosecution of those alleged responsible for crimes concerning the international community, he remains reticent upon the question of amnesty by declaring, in one of his famous article entitled: "The Amnesty exception to the Jurisdiction of the International Criminal Court" (1999), "that peace and justice are sometimes incompatible goals." Then, he concludes "that the existence of international criminal court does not remove amnesty as bargain chip." He is supported by (Elizabeth Ludwin King, 2010) who argues that "an amnesty must be necessary to end the conflict." But in this context, Elizabeth mentions that "an amnesty must be fair to all parties involved, and must be narrowly tailored to the particular context". Furthermore, there is a view mitigates on the meaning of interest of justice. According to (Kate Allan, 2020) "The Pre-Trial Chamber is not best placed to determine or define an international norm regarding conditional amnesties, which it would inevitably do if it makes judicial determinations regarding whether the amnesties are in the interests of justice." Although, Kate Allan argues that amnesty is inconsistent with the States' intention in enacting the Rome Statute, her opinion is remains mitigates on the

---

"*Powers and Duties of the Prosecutor*, "*in The Rome Statute of the International Criminal Court: A Commentary*, edited by Antonio Cassese, Paola Gaeta & John R.W.D. Jones (Oxford: oxford University press, 2002), P. 1142 (He expressed that the Prosecutor of ICC is a *"judicial, non-political organ, with no political legitimation and liability...");* also *see* Talita De Souza Dias, *International Criminal Court and Tribunals, "Interests of Justice": Defining the scope of Prosecutorial Discretion in Article 53 (1) (c) and 53 (2) (c) of the Rome Statute of International Criminal Court*, Leiden Journal of International Law, vol. 30, pp. 731-751.

[5] Kate Allan, Prosecution and Peace: *A Role for Amnesty Before the ICC?* 39 Denv.J. Int'l L. & Pol'y 239 (2019).

conditional. This demonstrates that Kate supports Elizabeth. But then, Giuliano Turone argues that it is the power and duties of the Prosecutor of the ICC to investigate and prosecute those atrocities. Further, (Giuliano Turone, 2002) asserts: "[t]he Prosecutor of International Criminal Court is a "judicial, non-political organ, with no political legitimation and liability, [...]." He expresses that to not proceed with the investigation, or prosecution would be an insult to the memory of victims. He has a rude position similar to Martin Macpherson who addressed an open letter to the Prosecutor of ICC, in 2005, on the meaning of the phrase "the interests of justice" in the provisions of Articles 53(1)(c) and (2)(c). To solve that controversial question, (Talita De Souza Dias, 2017) attempts, in addition, to give a legal interpretation of those Articles. According to him, the provisions of article 53 of the Rome Statute of ICC contain an "evidentiary test" which authorizes an initiation of investigation, or prosecution under articles 53(1) (c) (2) (c). This argumentation entirely supports the comparative analysis of (Chris Gallavin, 2003) upon the issue. Chris Gallavin considers those forms of alternative justice as an application for a domestic "public interest". In this context, he argues: "the application of domestic public interest for interests of justice is grossly inadequate and inappropriate within the International Criminal Court". He adds: "[w]hile being appropriate for application within a domestic system are entirely inappropriate for application within an international regime." At this effect, this thesis attempts to solve that legal issue by rationally adopting a theoretical approach. Under Article 53 of the Rome Statute, "the prosecutor has important responsibility to decide..." "whether to initiate an investigation, and, upon investigation, to decide..." "that there is not a sufficient basis for a prosecution."[6] So, before "making these decisions" the prosecutor shall focus on the fundamental element of this article that is the "interests of justice." This insinuates that the prosecutor office "may not fail to initiate an

[6] Rome Statute, Art. 53.

investigation, or decide not to proceed with investigation" on the grounds of ongoing peace processes such as national efforts, truth commissions, national amnesty[7], or traditional reconciliation methods. Thus, it is crucial to remember that the terms "interests of justice" were firstly included "in the August 1997 session of the Preparatory Committee in what became Article 53 at the initiative of groups working on behalf of victims, including the women's Caucus for Gender Justice, and Like-Minded Countries which were concerned that prosecutorial decisions, according to the language of the August 1996 report of the Prepatory Committee, report and compilation of proposals, not to investigate or prosecute crimes under the interests of justice ground would overlook the interests and rights of victims."[8]However, these alternative political methods, or justice mechanisms would entirely be contrary to the "object and purpose of the Rome Statute."

While the language of this concept "is not clear," the question of deterrence regarding the serious international crimes continues to weigh on international criminal law; which then permits perpetrators to be shielded from impunity on behalf of alternative justice methods.[9] For instance, this is the case with Ugandan President Yoweri Museveni in 2000, who offered amnesty to "soldiers from rebel group, the Lord's Resistance Army (LRA), who laid down their weapons. "In Uganda," the LRA has been fighting the Ugandan government for decades, often through the use of chilling tactics: "abducting children and turning the girls into sex slaves and the boys into drug-

---

[7] The term "amnesty" is derived from the Greek word "amnestia," which means forgetfulness or oblivion. Amnesty is an act of sovereign power "decriminalizing" a past offense. *See* Michael P. Scharf, *The Letter of the Law: The Scope of the International Legal Obligation to Prosecute Human Rights Crimes*, 59 LAw & CoNTEMP. PROBS. n1, (1996).

[8] *See* Amnesty International, "Open Letter to the Chief Prosecutor of the International Criminal Court: Comments on the Concept of the Interests of justice", drafted by Martin Macpherson, senior director of the International Law and Organizations Program, 17 June 2005.

[9] Kristin Henrard, The Viability of National Amnesties in View of the Increasing Recognition of Individual Criminal Responsibility at International Law, 8 *MSU-DCL J. Int'l L.* 595, 646 (1999). *See* also Denakpon L Tchobo, Tension between Peace and Justice under ICC: *Influence of Alternative Justice Mechanisms*, LLM note, pp. 26-28. (2019).

addled child soldiers. Abductees are forced to mutilate, maim, rape, and kill under penalty of death."[10] In this respect, the exercise of "prosecutorial discretion" regarding the "interests of justice" still raises a colossal issue under the ICC, like this was under the International Criminal Tribunals for Yugoslavia, Rwanda, and Special Court for Sierra Leone. In this sense, "any state amnesty provisions must be considered void if they attempt to cover the most serious international crimes such as: genocide, war crimes, crimes against humanity and other serious violations of international humanitarian law." [11]

In fact, we need a legal status with regard to "human rights abuses" perpetrators. The probing question: "why is there an ambiguity on the legal interpretation of the provisions of Article 53 of the Rome Statute?" suggests that the absence of a coherent answer on the concept of "the interests of justice" does leave a windows open for a new theoretical approach. The enormous challenge of this thesis is to enforce the mechanisms applicable to the concept of the "interests of justice" under the Rome Statute with regard to serious international crimes, by illuminating the ambiguity created by Articles 53 (1) (c) and 53 (2) (c) of this statute[12] in benefit of victims for an enforcement of justice consequent upon a breach of substantive international criminal law. Indeed, the endeavor is an arduous academic task attempting to save "the interests of victims," through the "obligation

---

[10] Int'l Crisis Grp, Northern *Uganda: Seizing the Opportunity for Peace*, 5 (Africa *Report No. 124*, April 26, 2007). The case of prosecution on the North of Uganda 29 July 2004 available on http:// www.icc-cpi-cpi.int/press/pressreleases.html (Accessed on April, 7, 2020).

[11] *See* Human Rights Watch (HRW), *The Meaning of ''the Interests of Justice'' In Article 53 of the Rome Statute*, Policy Paper, (June 2005) at p. 12; also *see* Diane Orentlicher, "Settling Accounts: *The Duty to Prosecute Human Rights Violations of a Prior Regime* ", (1991) 100 Yale Law Journal 2537.

[12] *Supra* note 5.

to protect" human dignity, in light of legal instruments related to international human rights law and international humanitarian law.[13]

This thesis attempts "to make a contribution to scholarship in the area of international criminal law" by applying a legal theory to the Rome Statute of International Criminal Court. Additionally, it challenges the accepted traditional practice-scholarship in relation to international law by opting- out of these complex practices, and setting up a new methodology which is considerably theoretical in its approach. The analysis is led under the governs of Article 21[14] of the Rome Statute and, through some international scholarship works, towards a doctrinal theory tending to substantially enforce objective views.

II-Purpose

The quarrel about the scope of Articles 53(1)(c) and 53 (2)(c) over the phrase "the interests of justice," regarding peace verses justice under amnesties in detriment to victims, paves the way for an interesting topic that will be the main focus of this thesis. It evaluates the symbol of balance

---

[13] *See supra* note 1, Principle 3.; also see ICCSt. Preamble. *("**Mindful** that during this century millions of children, women and men have been victims of unimaginable atrocities that deeply shock the conscience of humanity, **recognizing** that such grave crimes threaten the peace, security and well-being of the world.").*

[14] *See* Art. 21 ICCSt.

1. The Court shall apply:
    (a) In the first place, this Statute, Elements of Crimes and its Rules of Procedure and Evidence;
    (b) In the second place, where appropriate, applicable treaties and the principles and rules of international law, including the established principles of the international law of armed conflict;
    (c) Failing that, general principles of law derived by the Court from national laws of legal systems of the world including, as appropriate, the national laws of States that would normally exercise jurisdiction over the crime, provided that those principles are not inconsistent with this Statute and with international law and internationally recognized norms and standards.
2. The Court may apply principles and rules of law as interpreted in its previous decisions.
3. The application and interpretation of law pursuant to this article must be consistent with internationally recognized human rights, and be without any adverse distinction founded on grounds such as gender as defined in article 7, paragraph 3, age, race, colour, language, religion or belief, political or other opinion, national, ethnic or social origin, wealth, birth or other status.

within the international criminal justice system. Further, it analyses some gaps that exist within core crimes of the Rome Statute of ICC in favor of the protection of humanity.

III-Research Questions

In developing the research questions for this thesis, it is important to observe the efficiency of International Criminal Court in the race of deterrence for the protection of humanity within international criminal justice system. Establishing to put an end to the gravest atrocities concerning the international community, International Criminal Court is confronted to some provisions of its statute, which are Articles 53 (1) (c) and 53 (2) (c). However, as pointed out in the literature, the Office of Prosecutor may or may not initiate an "investigation" or "prosecution" on behalf of the concept of "interests of justice." In this perspective, the first issue that must be addressed is:

1. *Where is the sense of the justice if the Office of Prosecutor "may not, initiate an investigation," or "decide not to prosecute," in cases of the gravest international crimes, on behalf of interests of justice? And what is the real legal language of this concept?*

As it will be shown, many scholars, although the list is not exhaustive, attempt to touch the quintessence of this concept through theories based on the realist, ethical, and fundamental principles of law.[15] These questions are addressed in Part 1, where the concept of the "interests of justice" is structured in its legal spirit.

---

[15] *See supra* note 4.

2. *Could we analyze the Rome Statute, or some of its provisions in absence of international human rights law and international humanitarian law? Or could the object and purpose of international treaty be ineffective, because of one, or some of provisions of this treaty? In addition, where is the obligation to protect human dignity as being proclaimed by United Nations in Universal Declaration of Human Rights of 1948?*

In Part II, it is crucial to consider other international legal instruments protecting human rights. This thesis challenges the traditional of Article 53 by addressing its application in its effective and efficient normative goals.

3. *What does the Vienna Convention require, when some provisions of conventions, or international treaties raise complex issues in their applicability? If states breach their international legal obligations, how might victims be protected? What are the principles and rules of law that should be applied?*

Part III of this dissertation attempts to narrow the plain meaning of Article 53 to the Vienna Convention.[16] It rationally proposes mechanisms based on principles and rules of criminal law for the protection of victims. In addition, it attempts to enforce the substantive breach of international criminal law.

[16] As regards treaty interpretation, one would not look to "the preparatory work of the treaty and the circumstances of its conclusion" except to "confirm "the meaning reached from considering, among other things: (i) the ordinary meaning of the treaty in context and in light of its object and purpose; and (ii) relevant rules of international law, or where the meaning is ambiguous or leads to a result "which is manifestly absurd or unreasonable. "Vienna Convention, Art.32.

IV-Dissertation Outline

In consideration of these research questions, it is, undoubtedly, apparent that this thesis respects a linear development. In this way, it permits the reader to observe how, the victims of serious and most serious international crimes are overlooked, their rights are buried under this famous Article 53 of the Rome Statute. In addition, the reader should expect a theoretical approach permitting to clarify the ambiguity raised by this article, as well as a theory attempting to enforce the international criminal law. The thesis is divided into three parts.

Part I consists specifically of two chapters. Chapter 1 presents an overview on ICC; and then on the reprieve of investigations. Chapter 2 depicts the consideration of legal concepts that motivates this project, which is crucial in the understanding of the approach taken throughout. Part II comprises of a substantial analysis that is indubitably theoretical in the approach of this thesis. Chapter 3 analyses the spirit of Article 53 of the Rome Statute which is the ambiguous concept "interests of justice," and attributes a legal view through the different theories constituting the basic of law. Chapter 4 outlines the core crimes in the Rome Statute of the International Criminal Court with their gaps affecting the protection of human rights. It defends the interests of victims under each of those crimes. Further, it intends to enforce the Genocide Convention by proposing a legal framework to its effect. It addresses prosecutorial discretion in its legal context in light of international legal instruments. In Part III, chapter 5 tries to elucidate the ambiguity of provisions of Articles 53(1)(c) and 53 (2)(c) in light of the Vienna Convention on Law of Treaties. It exposes, moreover, the indispensable key factors of those provisions for effective "investigation and prosecution" of most serious international crimes within the jurisdiction of ICC. Chapter 6 attempts to bring together the analysis and findings of the entire dissertation with recommendations as support.

CHAPTER 1: OVERVIEW ON ICC

The International Criminal Court is a permanent international organ that is competent to judge natural persons,[17]suspected of crimes within its jurisdiction such as: crimes against humanity, war crimes, genocide and crime of aggression.[18] It is established on the ground that "*during this century millions of children, women and men have been victims of unimaginable atrocities that deeply shock the conscience of humanity.*"[19]

I-The Competences Of The Court

The ICC has basic competence to pursue any individual suspected of gross human rights abuses. It "shall have no jurisdiction over any person who was under the age of 18 at the time of the alleged commission of a crime."[20] Additionally, its competence is limited to four levels of international crimes. The ICC can judge in a geographic context as well as within an appropriate time period by respecting "the principle of complementarity" for the interests of justice. It can even be competent over crimes "committed on the territory of a State not party to the Rome Statute." In other words, those competences of the Court are named: "Ratione materiae," "ratione temporis," "ratione loci," and "ratione personae."

A-Subject Matter Jurisdiction: Ratione Materiae

The competence "ratione materiae" of ICC is related to the four substantive crimes falling into its jurisdiction namely: genocide, crimes against humanity, war crimes and the crime of

[17]Rome Statute, *supra* note 2, Art. 25.
[18] *Id.* at Art. 5.
[19] *Supra* note 2.
[20] Rome Statute, *supra* note 2, Art. 26, 27-28.

aggression.[21] According to the preamble of the Rome Statute those crimes are classified as the most serious crimes of concern to the International Community, the crimes are "unimaginable" atrocities that deeply shock the conscience of humanity.

B-The Temporary Competence of ICC: Ratione Temporis

First, "the Court may exercise its jurisdiction only with respect to crimes of aggression committed one year after the ratification or acceptance by thirty states parties." Its "ratione temporis" competence is exercised "only with respect to crimes committed after the entry into force of this statute." In other words, the ICC cannot have jurisdiction over the crimes committed prior July 1, 2002.[22] It has a principle of non-retroactivity- "ratione personae"; meaning, "No person shall be criminally liable for conduct prior to entry into force of the Statute making the Statute prospective."[23] For instance, in the Lubanga case, "the Pre-Trial Chamber I emphasized the issue of temporal application of the Statute… In conformity with article 126 (1)...the second condition would be met pursuant to article 11 of the Statute if the crimes underlying the case against Mr. Thomas Lubanga Dyilo were committed after 1 July 2002..., the Chamber considers that the second condition has also been met."[24] Moreover, this competence disposes an exception to the general rule with regard to the application of the Statute. Here, a state can make ad hoc declaration by recognizing the Court's jurisdiction over specific crimes, even though the state is not a party to the Statute;[25] such declarations, formulated in accordance with Article 12(3) of the statute, would appear to be retroactive by their very nature. This was the case when Uganda made

---

[21] Rome Statute, Art.5.
[22] *Id.* at Art. 11.
[23] Rome Statute, Art. 24. (The Court is not retroactive).
[24] *See* Charles O. Olubokun, *The Future of Prosecutions under the International Criminal Court*, p.26, PhD Thesis, Brunel University London, April (2015).
[25] Rome Statute, Art. 12 (3).

a "Declaration on Temporal Jurisdiction", by accepting the competence of the Court over the crimes committed on its territory following the entry into force of the Statute on 1 July 2002. Thus, the Pre-Trial Chamber III implied this declaration, and then confirmed the arrest warrant against Joseph Kony.[26] It is important to outline that there is difference between Jurisdiction "ratione temporis" and the "retroactive crimes."[27]

C-Jurisdiction Territorial: *Ratione Loci*

It is evident to mention that the Court is only competent for exercising its jurisdiction over the State Parties to Rome Statute. Where the State of alleged perpetrator is party to the Rome Statute , or if the crime is committed within territory of another State party, the Court may exercise its jurisdictional competence.[28] However, this is not a panacea for other States to continue to commit the gross violations of human rights within global society. The Court can exercise its jurisdiction over serious "crimes committed on the territory of State Parties regardless of the Nationality of the offender." Despite that, some States have not ratified the Rome Statute, the Court might have jurisdiction over those international crimes that occur within their territory. This justifies an exception to its competence, *ratione temporis*. In addition, the Court may directly exercise its jurisdiction on the request of a State which is not party to the Statute.[29] It may also react over a State not party to the Rome Statute on the request of United Nation Security Council. This is

---

[26] ICC-02/04-53 Warrant of Arrest for Joseph Kony Issued on 8 July 2005 amended on 27 September 2005 ¶32; ICC-02/04-54 Warrant of Arrest for Vincent Otti 8 July 2005 ¶32.

[27] William Schabas, *An introduction to the International Criminal Court* ,4th, CUP England, pp. 64-66 (2011).

[28] ICCSt, Art. 12 (2).

[29] Rome Statute, Art. 12 (2) (3).

related to the principle of referral.[30] In this respect, the State concerned complies with that decision because it is State member to the United Nations Charter.

Second, the ICC is limited with its principle of complementarity. It does not substitute to the domestic criminal justice system; it is just a complement.[31] Otherwise, the "ICC cannot prosecute the perpetrators where the state responsible, that has the internal competence, is investigating, or prosecuting the criminals accountable." But, if "the State concern is unable, unwilling, or reticent to prosecute the perpetrators, the ICC can do it."[32] So, the principle of complementarity exists for the respect of the principle of sovereignty of States.

D-Personal Jurisdiction: *Ratione Personae*

The competence "ratione personae" of the Court refers directly to individual criminal liability. In other words, the Statute provides that the ICC has jurisdiction only over natural persons;[33] and then those persons shall be of at least eighteen years of age at the time of the commission of the crime.[34] Contrarily to the customary international law under the ICJ, the Court does not recognize immunity in matter of prosecution of heads of state or officials identified as alleged perpetrators. This requires a "Cooperation with respect to waiver of immunity and consent to surrender." In this context, "[t]he Court may not proceed with a request for surrender or assistance which would require the requested State to act inconsistently with its obligations under

---

[30] *See* situation in Libya referred to ICC under the U.N. S.C./Res. 1970 (2011), also situation in Darfur, Sudan referred by the Security Council to ICC in March 2005; available at https://www.how-the-icc-works.aba-icc.org/cases/2011-unsc-resolution-on-libya-referral/ (Last visited October 1, 2020 at 7:21 P.M.).

[31] Rome Statute, *supra* note 2, Art.1.

[32] Rome Statute, Art. 1 and 16.

[33] Rome Statute, Art. 25(1).

[34] Rome Statute, Art.26.

international law with respect to the State or diplomatic immunity of a person or property of a third State, unless the Court can first obtain the cooperation of that third State for the waiver of the immunity."[35]Furthermore, it "may not proceed with a request for surrender which would require the requested State to act inconsistently with its obligations under international agreements pursuant to which the consent of a sending State is required to surrender a person of that State to the Court, unless the Court can first obtain the cooperation of the sending State for the giving of consent for the surrender."[36]

II- Legal Nature Of Reprieve Under ICC

"Sacred principle" of the International Criminal Court is crystallized on the negation of impunity, as well as on the accountability of international crimes. But, it should be noted that the Rome Statute is accepted in its practice as an alternative form of justice, with regard to provisions of Article 53, under the concept of the "interests of justice."[37] In effect, amnesties should be considered by the ICC in circumstances where the attenuation of sentence may or may not be necessary a handicap for "the interests of victims" and the international community.

As mentioned above, the Court was created to put an end to impunity and not for substituting alternative methods such as amnesty and truth commission, which constitutes an exit for criminals accountable to evade retribution. Indeed, amnesty is defined as: "the act of an authority (such as a government) by which pardon is granted to a large group of individuals."[38]It is officially pardoning someone before a trial or conviction. Its antonyms are penalty, retribution or

---

[35] Rome Statute, Art. 98(1).
[36] Rome Statute, Art. 98 (2).
[37] *Id.* at Art. 53(1) (c).
[38] *See* Merriam Webster online dictionary, available at https://www.merriam-webster.com/dictionary/amnesty.

punishment.[39] Etymologically, it is borrowed from Latin *amnēstia* what means "forgetfulness, oblivion, deliberate overlooking of past offenses."[40] Furthermore, the limits of ICC may also be analyzed with regard to the reprieve of investigation under the Rome Statute which requires suspension of prosecutions in favor of international peace with regard to the provisions of Articles 16 (1) and Article 17 (2), relating to the inadmissibility of case, and Article 20 (3) and (4) which permits the prosecutor to decide to not initiate an investigation.

A-The Reprieve Of Investigation Under Article 16

Article 16 permits the Office of the Prosecutor to abstain from prosecuting the States that settle a peace agreement with alternative justice methods through international recognition. In this circumstance, the Security Council demands ICC, in light of the Rome Statute, to drop the investigations, or the prosecution for twelve months.[41] This request may be renewed, and must be a resolution voted by Security Council in accordance with the Chapter VII of United Nations Charter, titled "Action with respect to threats to the peace, breaches of peace, and acts of aggression… peace, rupture of peace and acts of aggression."

However, it is important to question whether the Security Council is contradicting the overall objective of the UN Charter. The answer seems affirmative when we glance at popular views of critics which point out that "customary international law and the principle of *jus cogens* prohibit broadly actions that prevent prosecution of crimes under international law. This means

[39] *Id.*
[40] *Id.*
[41] Rome Statute, Article 16 (Any investigation, or prosecutions can be initiated for twelve months under the Rome Statute following the date of resolution adopted by Security Council in light of UN Charter's Chapter VII. This request can be renewed by the Security Council, but in the same condition).

that there is not yet a customary international law rule requiring prosecution of war crimes in internal armed conflict or crimes against humanity, but that there is a << duty>> to prosecute in the case of grave breaches of the Geneva Conventions, the crime of genocide, and torture."[42] After deeply analyzing it is very important to be curious on the word << *duty*>> and the contrast with the word <<*obligation*>>. Whence the debate on "duty" versus "obligation" is needed. But here is not the right place to tackle that; however, the absence of that obligation mentioned above in the quotation gave birth to the international criminal justice system from Nuremberg Tribunals up to the creation of ICC.

As a result, State Parties should not grant amnesties for the gravest international crimes such as genocide, crimes war, crimes against humanity, torture. This might constitute a form to legitimate the impunity of those crimes. To sum up, the United Nations Security Council intervention in the prosecution of the gravest international crimes should only be effective in referral situations.

B-Inadmissibility Under Article 17

Moreover, under the principle of complementarity ICC may declare a case inadmissible where it has been, or is being investigated or prosecuted by the State that has jurisdiction over it or if the State is unwilling or unable to genuinely investigate or prosecute.[43] Additionally, in the case where the proceedings would not be being conducted in an impartial or independent manner, or in any other manner "inconsistent with intent to bring the person to justice." [44] The test for

[42] *See* Michael P. Scharf, An Essay on Trading Justice for Peace, 63 Washington and Lee Law Review 339-376, (2006).
[43] Rome Statute, Art.17 (1) (a).
[44] Rome Statute, Art.17 (2) (c).

"unwillingness" occurs. According to Kleffner "unwillingness" refers to the "purpose" for which proceedings are undertaken, along with the "intent" of a State. This includes an evaluation of a state's subjective motivations hidden behind such proceedings.[45]

As a matter of fact, the question of inadmissibility and principle of complementarity is ambiguous. Complementarity is the principle for which the ICC completes domestic justice, but it does not override the domestic penal system. When a State can really exercise its jurisdictional competence and is determined to or able to genuinely prosecute the case within the national jurisdiction system, the ICC shall declare its inadmissibility. The principle of complementarity is governed by Article 17, and then is completed by Articles 18 as well as 19. Article 17 draws the substantives "tests of admissibility"; whereas Article 18 covers the preliminary "decisions of admissibility". Article 19 touches the later admissibility. In this respect, these alternative forms of justice could constitute a prejudice to the prosecution under the Rome Statute, either when the prosecutor's office initiates an investigation according to Article 18, or during the investigation and the prosecution. Regarding its procedure, this article explains that the prosecutor's office has to inform any competent State concerned about the investigation initiated in order to allow the State to override the ICC. Thus, the concerned State has one month for informing the prosecutor's office that is investigating over criminal acts in question, and then could require to the Prosecutor to suspend his investigation.[46]

In this case, when there is not a special authorization for the Court, the Office of the Prosecutor must give a reprieve in benefit of the State's investigation. Furthermore, the Office of

---

[45] Kleffner, *The Impact of Complementarity on National Implementation of Substance International Criminal Law*, 1 Journal of International Criminal Justice, p 86 (2003).

[46] Rome Statute, Art. 18 (2).

the Prosecutor may request updates regarding the investigations and prosecutions.[47] In other words, the Office of the Prosecutor has the ability, thereafter, to challenge a process of conditional amnesties or others alternative justice methods negotiated. Yet, it is crucial to understand that where the State concerned has competence over the gravest international crimes and does not ask the Office of the Prosecutor to suspend his or her investigation in a one-month delay, the reprieve period is automatically completed.

C-Ne Bis In Idem: Article 20

Article 20 of Rome Statute is based on "Ne bis in idem." This is a principle in which a person cannot be judged twice time for the same crime. In fact, it's a principle fundamentally, as well as constitutionally, recognized by all criminal justice systems. It is a general principle of criminal law. Then, the major question at this stage is whether Article 20 includes alternative, no jurisdictional methods such as amnesties. The response seems to be *NO* with regard to the language of Rome Statute.[48] Because Article 20 provides that for any jurisdiction cannot judge an accused *de novo* for an act already under prosecution of ICC. This is vice versa. A person cannot be tried twice time over the same crime. [49]However, the Court may exercise jurisdiction over the individual if the trial of perpetrators is not fair, or seems to shield the authors from impunity. In other words, the court can step in during situations "[where] the proceedings were not impartial or independent in accordance with internationally recognized standards of due process and in a manner insistent with an intention to bring the person to justice."[50] In this respect and by glancing

[47] Rome Statute, Art. 18.

[48] John Dugard, *Possible Conflicts of Jurisdiction with Truth Commissions*, *in The Statute de Rome*: Of The International Criminal Court: A commentary 700 (Antonio Cassese et al, ed., 2002).

[49] Rome Statute, Art. 20.

[50] Rome Statute, Article 20 (3) (b).

at the others alternative methods, it is crucial to mention that the word "justice" shall also include criminal liability.[51] So, Article 17 should not be in contrast with the article 20.

Conclusion

This chapter attempts to give a short literature review on the International Criminal Court. It also emphasizes some of these articles which might constitute a handicap for the effective protection of the interests of victims of crimes of the gravest violations of human rights. However, the chapters in infra would touch the main questions of this thesis, relating to the provisions of Article 53, as well as the gaps of international crimes within the jurisdiction of this Court which are detrimental to the interests of victims.

---

[51] *See* Carsten Stahn, *Complementarity, Amnesties and Alternative Forms of Justice*, 3 J. Int'l L Crim. Just. 695, 708 (The ambiguity existing in the statute favorites the recognition of some alternative methods according to the exceptional circumstance), pp 711- 716 (2005).

Chapter 2: Consideration Conceptual Of Justice

Access to justice should be a fundamental right naturally inherent to all human beings living within a community, or society regardless their race, sex, age, and religious considerations. Justice is perceived, objectively, in term of "truth"; and its principle is observed as the vindication of right over wrong.[52] In this regard, Dr. Arthur H. Garrison, Associate Professor of Criminal Justice at Kutztown University , has said : "Justice, in subjective terms, is defined by what ought to be or what should happen - whether the result is fair."[53] Furthermore, he defines justice "with a recognition that it is defined by what is done and achieved" "and then asserts : "[b]ecause God is a God of justice, justice is defined by what God is and, more importantly, justice is defined by what God does, how He does it, and why He does it."[54]

Though obvious, it is important to point out that this conceptual approach is based on a biblical authoritative which would wipe out the different beliefs under the universal rights of freedom. Instead of basing the definition on religion, the definition of justice should rather be based on an idea accepted by everyone. Hence, it would be acceptable to perceive the notion of justice as a process, or action seeking to protect the rights of victims as well as those presumed or accused, through a fair trial, for normative goals. In other words, the concept of justice must be the recognition of outcomes from social commitment; what the famous French Philosopher J.J.

---

[52] *See* Arthur H. Garrison, Defining the Meaning and Purpose of Justice, Law, and Criminal Justice: *A Hermeneutical Judeo-Christian Biblical Perspective*, 55 J. Cath. Leg. Stud. 1 at * 5. (2016).

[53] *See Id.* at *2 and *6.

[54] *Id.* (Emphasizing that the author defined the concept of justice by focusing on the Word of God, the Bible, such as Colossians 3:25 (NASB); 2 Thessalonians 1:8-10 (NKJV) ("Dealing out retribution to those who do not know God and to those who do not obey the gospel of our Lord Jesus. These will pay the penalty of eternal destruction, away from the presence of the Lord and from the glory of His power[.]")).

Rousseau[55] called "*The Social Contract*"[56]. In this perspective, the justice can never be effective without law.

While we are entirely aware that different systems of justice exist, this chapter assumes an analysis of its purpose under the criminal justice system which is the fundamental stone of international criminal law justice. However, the evidence examines the meaning of justice under the international criminal law; and its ethical operationalization through the principle of applied legality.[57]

I-The Meaning of Justice Under International Criminal Law

This section tackles the nature of international crimes and individual criminal responsibility. Both constitute the elements that construct an effective character of the international criminal justice system.

A-The Normative Dilemma: The Nature of Crimes

The normative dilemma is observed under a comparative analogy of domestic criminal justice systems and the international criminal law system; even though under the domestic criminal justice system there are some exceptions.[58]Indeed, under the Rome Statute there is no statute of

[55] French Philosopher and Writer 1712-1778, author of "The Social Contract".

[56] *Id.* This book edited in 1976 by this famous Philosopher is also called "*Principles of Political Rights*". (Rousseau demonstrated, in this book, that laws are binding only when they are accepted by the general will of the people).

[57] *See* Rome Statute Art. 22 and 23.

[58] Contrarily to the most of civil law countries where contraventions are limited to one year, offense three years, and crimes ten years, the United States maintains the principle of no limitation period of some crimes in accordance with 18 U.S.C. § 3299. "The felonies in Chapters 109A, 110 and 117 include violations of 18 U.S.C. 2241 For instance (aggravated sexual abuse), 2242 (sexual abuse), 2243 (sexual abuse of a ward or child), 2244 (abusive sexual contact), 2245 (sexual abuse resulting in death), 2250 (failure to register as a sex offender), 2251 (sexual exploitation of children), 2251A (selling or buying children), 2252 (transporting, distributing or selling child sexually exploitive material), 2252A (transporting or distributing child pornography), 2252B (misleading names on the Internet), 2260

limitation concerning international crimes. The Rome Statute of International Criminal Court provided that any crimes that fall into its jurisdiction shall not be subject to any statute of limitations.[59] The Rome Statute imported from the customary international law the spirit of the imprescriptibility of core crimes such as genocide and crimes against humanity, as well war crimes.[60] This may not be excluding the duty of State Parties regarding the investigation and prosecution;[61] but, it insinuates rather that their national laws should have no bearings on Article 53 related to investigation and prosecution of crimes within jurisdiction of the Court regardless of when they occurred.[62] However, the State's responsibility imposes a priori on itself under the international criminal law.

B-State Responsibility and Individual Criminal Accountability

Obviously, individual accountability is different from State responsibility. This difference obliges us to emphasize the notion of responsibility and culpability in international criminal law. In effect, "the duty to prosecute" or "extradite" is an international legal obligation of State concern under *Jus Cogens* norms. The rule of *Jus cogens* is "a peremptory norm" that is a fundamental principle of international law binding all the States that have accepted it as a norm.[63] It is accepted

(making child sexually exploitative [...]". *See* Charles Doyle, *Statute of Limitation in Federal Criminal Cases*, CRS Report RS21121, n18, p 2, Nov. 14 (2017) available at https://www.fas.org/sgp/crs/misc/RL31253.pdf.

[59] *See* Rome Statute Art. 29.

[60] *See* the Convention on the Non-Applicability of Statutory Limitations to War Crimes and Crimes Against Humanity, adopted on Nov. 26 (1968), available at https://www.un.org/en/genocideprevention/documents/atrocity-crimes/Doc.27_convention%20statutory%20limitations%20warcrimes.pdf.

[61] *See,* Michael P. Scharf, *supra* note 42.

[62] *See* Rome Statute, Art. 21(c). (However, the investigation and, or prosecution do not exclude the competence *temporis* of the Court).

[63] M.P. Scharf, *supra* note 42.

by all the States as *no derogatory* norm. Yet the notion of State responsibility could be identified under two angles as following:

First, the obligation to investigate crimes that occurred on the territory of States concerned and prosecute the perpetrators. This is a dual obligation of States concerned in the deterrence of international crimes. In this regard, ICC may declare a case inadmissible where it has been or is being investigated or prosecuted by a State that has jurisdiction over it, or if the State is unwilling or unable genuinely to investigate or prosecute.[64] But, in situations when the proceedings are not be being conducted in an impartial or independent manner or in any other manner inconsistent with intent to bring justice, this constitutes an evidence for a confirmation of State's "unwillingness."[65] By doing so, it is a question of the principle of complementarity under the Rome Statute. According to Kleffner, this test refers to the "purpose" for which proceedings are undertaken, and the "intent" of a State.[66] It is crucial to underscore that the principle of complementarity is governed by Article 17, and then is completed by Articles 18 and 19.[67] Article 17 draws the substantives tests of admissibility; whereas the article 18 covers the preliminary decisions of admissibility, and the article 19 touches the later admissibility as mentioned above. Meaning, when the State concerned is unable to turn in appropriate terms regarding Article 17, State has the duty to extradite the perpetrators with regard to international law.

Second, the obligation to extradite is the alternative international obligation of State concerned. The crimes under the Rome Statute were confined with a customary *erga omnes*, obligation upon

---

[64] Rome Statute, art. 17 (1)(a).
[65] Rome Statute, art. 17 (2) (c).
[66]*See*, Kleffner, *supra* note 45.
[67] Rome Statute.

States, and *aut dedere aut judicare* requiring to prosecute or extradite.[68] However, "there is no provision under the Rome Statute relating to the individual criminal responsibility that shall affect the responsibility of State under the international law."[69] In other words, the notion of individual criminal responsibility is directly related to the natural persons, alleged perpetrators of international crimes.[70]It exposes the criminal liability of perpetrators involved in the gross violation of human rights and serious violations of international humanitarian law falling into the jurisdiction of the Court. In this context, a person who commits a crime within the jurisdiction of the Court shall be individually responsible and liable for punishment in light of the Rome Statute.[71]In this respect, the individual's responsibility and liability shall criminally be determined, for the purpose of this Statute as following:[72]

> (a) Commits such a crime, whether as an individual, jointly with another or through another person, regardless of whether that other person is criminally responsible;
>
> (b) Orders, solicits or induces the commission of such a crime which in fact occurs or is attempted;
>
> (c) For the purpose of facilitating the commission of such a crime, aids, abets or otherwise assists in its commission or its attempted commission, including providing the means for its commission;

---

[68] *See* Diane Orentlicher, Settling Accounts: The Duty to Prosecute Human Rights Violations of a Prior Regime, (1991) 100 Yale Law Journal at* 2537.

[69] Rome Statute, art. 25 (4).

[70] Rome Statute, art. 25(1).

[71] *Id.* art. 25(2).

[72] *Id.* art. 25 (3).

(d) In any other way contributes to the commission or attempted commission of such a crime by a group of persons acting with a common purpose. Such contribution shall be intentional and shall either:

(i) Be made with the aim of furthering the criminal activity or criminal purpose of the group, where such activity or purpose involves the commission of a crime within the jurisdiction of the Court; or

(ii) Be made in the knowledge of the intention of the group to commit the crime;

(e) In respect of the crime of genocide, directly and publicly incites others to commit genocide;

(f) Attempts to commit such a crime by taking action that commences its execution by means of a substantial step, but the crime does not occur because of circumstances independent of the person's intentions.

However, it is important to mention with regard to the provision of Article 25 (3) (f) "[t]hat a person who abandons the effort to commit the crime or otherwise prevents the completion of the crime shall not be liable for punishment under this Statute for the attempt to commit that crime if that person completely and voluntarily gave up the criminal purpose".

II-Operationalization Ethical Of Principle Of Legality Applied

This section highlights the principle of *nullem crimen sine lege.*[73] In light of this legal principle, punishment under international criminal justice was, already, defined and locked. Thus,

[73] Rome Statute, Art.22.

it would be doubtful that the scope of Article 53 of ICCSt is perceived under alternative justice methods such as amnesty or national peace processes.

The double legal character[74] of international criminal law could be identified on one hand under the retribution, and on the other hand under the reparation. This insinuates that the concept of justice encompasses the retribution and the reparation, as double legal character, in consideration of the principle of legality under international criminal law.

A-The Retribution Under The International Criminal Law

The punishment of wrongdoings emerged and enlarged historically under international law as an aftermath of the happenings in Germany during World War II.[75] The jurisprudence of Nuremberg Tribunal was the trigger element of international criminal law.[76] In other words, the Nuremberg Charter and Judgment were the mother that gave birth to individual criminal responsibility under international law with regard to principle of *nullem crimen sine lege* (the equivalent to the U.S. Constitution's ex post facto law prohibition).[77] In effect, the notion of punishment was introduced in international criminal law to put an end to the gross violations of human rights within the civilized world.[78] The major justification of punishment was the deterrence aspect. But, this was strongly challenged by municipal jurisprudence.[79] Because, at the

---

[74] *See* Denakpon L. Tchobo, *Tension between Peace and Justice under ICC: Influence of Alternative Justice Mechanisms*, pp.28-29 (2019) (unpublished LL.M. note, Case Western Reserve University School of Law) (on file with author).

[75] Farooq Hassan, *The Theoretical Basis of Punishment in International Criminal Law,* 15 Case W. Res. J. Int'l L. 39, p 50. (1983).

[76] *Id.*

[77] *See* Michael P. Scharf, *How the War Against ISIS Changed International Law*, 48 Case W. Res. J. Int'l L. p 14. (2016).

[78] *See* Rome Statute, Preamble.

[79] *See*, Stone, *Hopes and Loopholes in the 1974 Definition of Aggression*, 71 AM. J. Int'l L. 224 (1977).

States level, municipal jurisprudence influence international crimes.[80]There are rules of humanitarian law, war crimes aggression by one State against another, the illegal use of certain kinds of weapons,[81] genocide,[82] and war crimes against humanity.[83] This justifies the approach regarding the notion of deterrence emphasized by Farooq Hassan[84] that was done under the so-called *Grotian Moment*[85]. This implicitly means that the non-efficiency of the application of the deterrence through the notion of punishment gave birth to the Rome Statute of International Criminal Court.[86] In this context, the creation of Rome Statute should be the panacea. But, unfortunately, it is confronted by the provisions of Article 53 under the famous concept of "the interests of justice." Thus, the major preoccupation is to wonder to what extent the ICC serves justice: whether the victims should be abandoned to their fate under this notion of the "interests of justice" or not? This constitutes a huge handicap to the victim's interests as well as to the deterrence of gravest human rights abuses today.

---

[80] *See*, Farooq Hassan, *supra* note 75 at pp.40-59; G.A. Res. 3314, 29 U.N. G.A.O.R. Supp. (No. 31) at 142, U.N. Doc. A/9631 (1974); *See* B. FERENCZ, *2 Defrn4ng International Aggression: The Search For World Peace,* 50- 53 (1975); Stone, *Hopes and Loopholes in the 1974 Definition of Aggression*, 71 AM. J. Int'l L. 224 (1977).

[81] *See* Convention on the Prohibition of the Development Production and Stockpiling of Bacteriological (Biological) and Toxic Weapons and on their Destruction, 27 U.N. G.A.O.R. Supp. (No. 30) at 17, U.N. Doc. A/8189 (1970); Geneva Protocol for the Prohibition of the Use in War of Asphyxiating, Poisonous or Other Gases of Bacteriological Methods of Warfare, Doc. C. 362 M. 135 1927 IX (1927); Treaty Banning Nuclear Weapon Tests in the Atmosphere, in Outer Space and Under Water, Aug. 5, 1963, 14 U.S.T. 1313, T.I.A.S. No. 5433; Treaty on the Prohibition of The Emplacement of Nuclear Weapons on the Sea Bed and The Ocean Floor and in the Sub-Soil Thereof, 25 U.N. G.A.O.R. Supp. (No. 28) at 11, U.N. Doc. A/8189 (1970); Treaty on Principles Governing the Activities of States in Exploration and Use of Outer Space, Including the Moon and Other Celestial Bodies, Jan. 27, 1967, 18 U.S.T. 2410, T.I.A.S. No. 6347; Antarctic Treaty, Dec. 1, 1959, 12 U.S.T. 794, T.I, S. No. 4780.

[82] *See,* Genocide Convention.

[83] *See* Bassiouni, *International Law and the Holocaust*, 9 CAL. W. INT'L L.J. 202 (1979).

[84] *See*, Farooq Hassan, *supra* note 75.

[85] *See,* Michael P. Scharf, *supra* note 61, at 13.

[86] *Id.*

B-The Reparation Of Rights Of Victims Under ICC

The notion of reparations[87] under ICC seems to be exported from the UN's "Basic Principles of Justice for Victims of Crime and Abuse of Power, and then the draft UN Basic Principles on the Right to Reparation". At the start, ICC does not implement under its Rules of Evidence and Procedure and the Regulations any specific principles regarding reparations.[88] Otherwise, the adoption of its official overall strategy as regards to rights of victims has been in effect since November 2009.[89] However the definition of victim, in absence from Rome Statute, is provided by Rule 85 of the Rules of Procedure and Evidence. In this Rule victims are defined as "natural persons" who have suffered harm as a result of the commission of any crime within the jurisdiction of the Court.[90] Furthermore, the notion of victims is expanded towards organizations or institutions, dedicated to religion, art, science, charitable or humanitarian purposes, as well as historic monuments and hospitals.[91]

Moreover, it is important to highlight that the Assembly of State Parties to the Rome Statute created a Trust Fund for victims and their families in 2002.[92] Because the notion of State responsibility does not exist under ICC, this organ is independently managed by the Assembly of State Parties. Additionally, the Trust Fund may receive voluntary contributions from other entities such as governments, international organizations, individuals, corporations and others.[93] But, that

---

[87] *See* Rome Statute, Art. 75(1).

[88] *See* Christine Evans, THE RIGHT TO REPARATION IN INTERNATIONAL LAW FOR VICTIMS OF ARMED CONFLICT, Cambridge University, p. 102 (2012).

[89] International Criminal Court, Report of the Court on the Strategy in Relation to Victims, 10 November 2009, ICC-ASP/8/45, ¶ 6. *See* discussion in Redress, 'Victims' Central Role in Fulfilling the ICC's Mandate', Paper for the 8th Assembly of States Parties, The Hague, 18–26 November 2009, available at: www.redress.org.

[90] ICC Rules of Procedure and Evidence, Adopted by the Assembly of States Parties, New York, 3–10 September 2002, Official Records ICC-ASP/1/3.

[91] Diane Orentlitcher , *supra* note 68.

[92] Rome Statute Art.79.

[93] *See*, Diane Orentitcher, *supra* note 68, p. 105.

principle does not depict the *de juro* rights of victims with regard to the concept of justice. Indeed, victims should have a specific statutory right, independent of the victim's participatory rights,[94] which might allow them to have a procedural standing in the process in order to trigger the jurisdiction of the Court under Article 15 (3) of the Rome statute.[95] In other words, victims deserve exceptionally direct access to the Appeals Chamber.[96] Keeping victims away from procedural standing would be a universal danger in detriment to the credibility of the Court. For instance, in cases of torture, rape, and sexual violence crimes, the victims have the right to be involved in the investigation proceedings all the way up to the Appeals chamber. Otherwise, how might the prosecutor trigger the jurisdiction of the Court in cases without all the parties?

For this concern, it would be appreciable to engage all the parties in the litigation at the start of investigation proceeding under Article 15 (3) and (4) in order to avoid the frequent appeal relating to the provisions of Article 15.[97]In this context, granting procedural rights to the victims from the investigation proceedings would be a substantial asset for the respect of human rights law, for the interests of justice, in light of the effectiveness of the justice. However, although the Rome Statute does not provide the legal meaning of the term "party" (not even in "the Rules of Procedure of Evidence or the Elements of Crimes"); it may, according to Judge Mindua, "[S]ometimes means either the prosecutor or the defense, and sometimes, it simply means any "participant" who has a personal interest in the judicial process, like the victims." [98] The most

[94] Rome Statute, Art. 68(3).
[95]This article provided that "[if] the Prosecutor concludes that there is a reasonable basis to proceed with an investigation, he or she shall submit to the Pre-Trial Chamber a request for authorization of an investigation, together with any supporting material collected. Victims may make representations to the Pre-Trial Chamber, in accordance with the Rules of Procedure and Evidence".
[96] *See* Amicus Curiae Observations Pursuant to Rule 103 of the Rules of Procedure and Evidence, ICC-02/17-5811 June 2019, ¶¶ 72-96.
[97] ICC-02/17-92, ¶ 31.
[98] Partially Dissenting Opinion of Judge Antoine Kesia-Mbe Mindua, ICC-02/17-62-Anx, 17 September 2019, ¶ 20. [Emphasis added].

important and indispensable word in that definition is: *the victims*; because, there is no justice without victims. In other words, victims are responsible for the prosecution. Their existence after commission of those crimes triggers the jurisdiction of the Court. Lack of their involvement, any justice would be etymologically void of substance. This would seem that the victims are an instrument of the Court.[99]

Conclusion

To sum up, as mentioned above, justice should be a process, or action seeking to protect the rights of victims as well as those presumed or accused through a fair trial, for normative goals. The implication of all the parties concerned in the process is indispensable for its double legal character in benefit of the ethical operationalization of the principle of legality[100]. Otherwise, it would be incomprehensible to highlight the notion of reparation of rights of victims without considering their existence in the triggering jurisdiction of the Court. Victims being out, in favor of any amnesty, might be considered discrimination to their regard, which furthers the violation of human rights under the Rome Statute of International Criminal Court.

[99] *See* S. Kendall and S. Nouwen, *Representational Practices at the International Criminal Court: The Gap Between Juridified and Abstract Victimhood*, 76 Law and Contemporary Problems, 235-262, at 258 (2014); K.M. Clarke, *Fictions of Justice: The ICC and the Challenge of Legal Pluralism in Sub-Saharan Africa*, Cambridge University Press, pp. 20-23 (2009); R. Killean and L. Moffett, *Victim Legal Representation before the ICC and* ECCC, 15 JICJ, pp.713-740 (2017).

[100] Rome Statute, Art. 22.

PART II- ANALYSIS AND EVALUATION

CHAPTER 3: THE SPIRIT OF ARTICLE 53 OF ICCST

I-The Scope Of Discretionary Power

A-Ineluctable Relationship Between Articles 53 (1) (C) And 53 (2) (C)

At this level, analysis is effective under the consideration of theoretical approach done by some scholars[101] who have also attempted to clarify the ambiguity of this article. Indeed, Article 53(1) (c) stipulates that "[t]aking into account the gravity of the crime and the interests of victims, there are nonetheless substantial reasons to believe that an investigation would not serve the interests of justice." Furthermore, regarding Article 53 (2) (c): "[a] prosecution is not in the interests of justice, taking into account all the circumstances, including the gravity of the crime, the interests of victims and the age or infirmity of the alleged perpetrator, and his or her role in the alleged crime". The provisions of this article depict the discretion power of the prosecutor with the aim to prosecute individuals responsible for crimes of the gravest concern to the international community.[102] They first draw on, the power of *affirmative duty* [103]of prosecutor permitting him or her to initiate an investigation upon legal considerations, and secondly, they draw on the power of *no affirmative duty*[104] allowing to the prosecutor to *NOT* decide to investigate or prosecute for

[101] *See* Talita De Souza Dias, *International Criminal Court and Tribunals "Interests of Justice: Defining the scope of Prosecutorial discretion in Article 53 (1) (c) and (2) (c) of the Rome Statute of International Criminal Court*, Leiden J Int'l L. 30, pp. 731-751. (2017).

[102] *See* Preamble ICCSt. ¶¶ 4-5.

[103] The power of affirmative duty is the use of discretion of prosecutor to initiate an investigation, or decide to prosecute the gravest international crimes in benefit of victims. When s/he uses that discretion to *Not* investigate, or prosecute in consideration of some factors for the interests of justice, this might regard as the exercise of her/his power of "no affirmative duty". Otherwise, the prosecutorial discretion depicts two powers the "affirmative duty" and the "not affirmative duty".

[104] *Id.*

the "interests of justice." Although, both powers represent entirely the discretion power of the prosecutor of the Court in the criminal investigation, these provisions raise a problem of ambiguity through the lack an explicit legal definition.[105] That ambiguity stimulates a divergence of views within scholarship academic community.[106] Some regarded this ambiguity of this provisions, under the *no affirmative duty*, as an alternative form of justice such as amnesties, pardons, truth and reconciliation commissions, and on goings of peace and security.[107] According to Kate Allan, "[a]mnesty is a persuasive bargaining chip."[108] It "can be a useful bargaining chip in peace negotiations".[109] This may be an asset of deterrence for the prosecutor to constrain perpetrators from disarming on the ground that they pose a real threat of arrest.[110] But then, other views narrow the sense of the interests of justice to the key factors of those provisions such as: "gravity of crimes, interests of victims, the age or infirmity of the accused, and his or her role in the alleged crime," which exclude those alternative forms of justice.[111]Thus, granting amnesty on the ground of the interests of justice under Article 53 is in dichotomy with the purpose and goal of Rome Statute preamble of ICC.[112] Amnesty may be acceptable under the domestic law; but should not have judicial effect over the international criminal law system in case of serious international crimes. Moreover, according to the Inter-American Commission on Human Rights, amnesties violate the

---

[105]See William A. Schabas and Ramesh Thakur, ATROCITIES AND INTERNATIONAL ACCOUNTABILITY: *Beyond Transitional Justice*, United Nations University Press, pp.143-145 (2007); Andreas O'Shea, AMNESTY FOR CRIME IN INTERNATIONAL LAW AND PRACTICE, Kluwer International Law, p. 317 (2002).

[106]*See*, T. De Souza, *supra* note 86, at 732.

[107]*See* Elizabeth B. Ludwin King, *Amnesties In A Of Time Of Transition*, 41 Geo. Wash. Int'l L. Rev. 577, at** 617-618 (2010).

[108]Kate Allan, *supra* note 5, at *288.

[109]*Id.*

[110]*See*, Michael P. Scharf, *supra* note 42, p 342.

[111]*See* M. Macpherson, *Comments on the concept of the interests of justice*, Amnesty International, Open Letter to the Chief Prosecutor of the International Criminal Court, Jun. 17 (2005); C. Gallavin, *Article 53 of The Rome Statute of The International Criminal Court: In the Interests of Justice?* 14 King's College Law Journal 179, at 193-197 (2003). (According to Gallavin "amnesty" is an application for a "domestic public interests"; and not for interests of justice in international regime).

[112] Diane, *supra* note 53.

rights to remedy and to due process in the American Convention.[113]

Indeed, the effectiveness of Article 53 requires a certain evaluation of those provisions with regard to crimes committed. The reason why, Talita De Souza has said: "[t]he relevance of Article 53(1)(a)–(b) and (2)(a)–(b) lies in the way in which those provisions operate in relation to Article 53(1)(c) and (2)(c). In fact, the assessments or tests contained in subparagraphs (a), (b) and (c) in both paragraphs 1 and 2 appear to be listed as a logical sequence of steps. In this sense, if the prosecutor has reached the 'interests of justice' test in Article 53(1)(c) or (2)(c), he or she must have already concluded that the tests contained in paragraphs 1(a)–(b) and 2(a)–(b) would authorize the initiation of an investigation or prosecution, respectively".[114] This assertion encourages us to support this scholar on the existence of "evidentiary test". This means there is sufficient information on the commission of crimes under Articles 53 (1) (a) or (2) (a).[115] In this context, it would be incomprehensible to use the power of *no affirmative duty* in detriment to victims. Because the most serious crimes of international concern might never exist without evidence. The evidence is always palpable and non-contradictory under a logic tending towards culpability or criminalization of natural persons. So, the prosecutor should conclude under the provisions of Article 53 (1)(c) and (2)(c) that these crimes fall within jurisdiction of the Court; and then deserve to be investigated and prosecuted.[116] That power should be used in favor of Article 53 (4) which allows the prosecutor to reconsider any of his or her decisions under paragraphs 1 and 2 based on new facts or information.[117]

---

[113] Herrera v. Argentina, Cases 10.147, 10.181, 10.240, 10.262, 10.309, & 10.311, Inter-Am. Comm'n H.R., Report No. 28/92, OEA/Ser.L./ V/II.83, doc. 14, corr. 1 (1993); Masacre Las Hojas v. El Salvador, Case 10.287, Inter-Am. Comm'n H.R., Report No. 26/92, OEA/Ser.L./V/II.83, doc. 14, corr. 1 (1992-93) [hereinafter El Salvador Case];
De Los Santos Mendoza v. Uruguay, Cases 10.029, 10.036, 10.145, 10.305, 10.372, 10.373, 10.374, &10.375, Inter-Am. Comm'n H.R., Report No. 29/92, OEA/Ser.L./V/II.83, doc. 14, corr. 1 (1993) [hereinafter Uruguay Cases].

[114] T. De Souza, *supra* note 101, p 743.

[115] *Id.*

[116] Rome Statute, Art.1.

[117] *See* T. De Souza, at 744.

B-The Protection Of Human Rights

The obligation to protect human dignity is crucial. There is no justice without victims. In plain language, the ICC was established because, victims existed. That is to say the existence of these victims of the gravest atrocities over the past two decades forced the founders to think about the stability of humanity for peace and international security. However, it would be incomprehensible to trade them away in oblivion. To be aware, *de facto*, of the psychology of the civilized world, it is absolutely necessary to outline the unacceptable pattern that alters the interests of victims to amnesty. For instance in Uganda case, the so-called Lord of Armed (LRA), Joseph Kony and his members, allegedly committed war crimes (including murder, cruel treatment of civilians, intentionally directing an attack against a civilian population, pillaging, inducing rape, and forced enlistment of children,) and crimes against humanity, (including murder, enslavement, sexual enslavement, rape, and inhumane acts of inflicting serious bodily injury and suffering). The LRA wanted an amnesty in detriment to the victims[118] during negotiations resulting in a peace agreement, which began in Juba on July 16th, 2006.[119] That reaction is absolutely in contrast with the respect and promotion of human rights under the international criminal law.

Indeed, the protection of human rights is influenced by the subjective meaning granted to the provisions of Article 53 (1) (c) (2) (c) of the Rome Statute under ICC. The Human Rights Committee addressed the legality of amnesties for human rights violations on several occasions by enforcing the International Covenant for Civil and Political Rights.[120] For the Committee forms of justice substituting the affirmative duty of the prosecutor such as amnesties are "generally

---

[118] *See supra* note 10. (Joseph Kony, a self-styled Christian prophet believed to be in his 40s, led the LRA has captured and enslaved more than 20,000 children, Kony and his members have raped many of the girls and brutally They forced the boys to serve as guerrilla soldiers).

[119] *See* Kate Allan, *supra* note 5, at **279-280.

[120] *See,* Elizabeth B. Ludwin King, *supra* note 107, at* 609.

incompatible" with the duty to investigate acts of torture.[121] Additionally, states have a duty to investigate and prosecute individuals who have committed war crimes and crimes against humanity.[122] According to The Human Rights Committee people who have committed war crimes or crimes against peace or humanity are ineligible for amnesty.[123]

II-Analyzing The Concept Of Interests Of Justice

Undoubtedly, victims should be in the heart of the justice. The double legal character should be the substance of justice in favor of victims. Respect to their memory must be indefectible, even when they die or pass away. As demonstrated above, the Rome Statute of International Criminal Court and International Humanitarian Law do not explicitly give the legal definition of term "victim." The absence of that legal definition obliges us to consider the legal meaning granted to the victims in the International Law. Indeed, under the UN Basic Principles, "victims" mean "persons who, individually or collectively, have suffered harm, including physical or mental injury, emotional suffering, economic loss or substantial impairment of their fundamental rights, through acts or omissions that are in violation of criminal laws operative within Member States,

---

[121] *See Id*, n179. [U.N. Human Rights Comm., Compilation of General Comments and General Recommendations Adopted by Human Rights Treaty Bodies, cmt. 20, P 15, U.N. Doc. HRI/GEN/1/Rev.1 (July 29, 1994). (Paragraph 15 states the following:

> The Committee has noted that some States have granted amnesty in respect of acts of torture. Amnesties are generally incompatible with the duty of States to investigate such acts; to guarantee freedom from such acts within their jurisdiction; and to ensure that they do not occur in the future. States may not deprive individuals of the right to an effective remedy, including compensation and such full rehabilitation as may be possible)].

[122] *See* G.A. Res. 2840 (XXVI), P 4, U.N. Doc A/8429 Dec.18, (1971) available at https://www.research.un.org/en/docs/ga/quick/regular/26 (Accessed on September 22, 2020).

[123] *See* G.A. Res. 3074 (XXVIII), P 1, U.N. Doc A/9030 Dec. 3, p5 (1973) available at https://www.un.org/en/genocideprevention/documents/atrocitycrimes/Doc.28_Principles%20of%20international%20cooperation%20in%20detection.pdf (Accessed on September 22, 2020). This Resolution provides that:" [p]ersons against whom there is evidence that they have committed war crimes and crimes against humanity shall be subject to trial and, if found guilty, to punishment, as a general rule in the countries in which they committed those crimes. In that connection, States shall co-operate on questions of extraditing such persons".

including those laws."[124] In the domestic system, victims have the right of participating in the whole process. In this perspective there are four stages that might grant this right to victims which reinstate their ownership of the conflict, allowing them to speak.[125] The first their involvement in the process to determine the culpability, or the guilt of the accused.[126] This step just opens the door to the three others. The second proposed step is the most "victim-centric." Victims have an opportunity to tell their story and recount the harm suffered and what restitution could make up for this harm.[127] The third stage is the sum of two first stages. It is the result of the sentence, or the condemnation. The last stage is the so-called *service rights* of the victim; it permits the victims to be informed of process updates of the sentence, fostering the rehabilitative value of the entire process.[128]

According to Yvonne McDermott, "[a]t least three of these four steps have been loosely followed in domestic criminal trials in some countries, which generally assess the guilt or innocence of the accused. If the accused is found guilty, the victims are offered an opportunity to present a victim impact statement, and then a sentence is imposed, taking the holistic set of circumstances into account".[129] However, the ICC adopted the participation of victims with regard to the Basic Principles model of participation. In this context, victims may present their *views* and *concerns* at an appropriate stage in the proceedings, in order to protect the right of the accused in favor of a fair and impartial trial. But, the rights of victim developed here is just a theory. Contrari

---

[124] See Article 1, UN Declaration of Basic Principles of Justice for Victims of Crime and Abuse of Power, adopted by UN General Assembly Resolution 40/34 of 29 November 1985, Annex (hereinafter, 'Basic Principles').

[125] *See* Yvonne MCDermott, *Victims And International Law: Remedies In The Courtroom*, Hague Justice Journal, 4 No. 3, P 199 (2009).

[126] *Id.*

[127] *Id.*

[128] *Id.*

[129] *Id.*

to the victim's participatory rights[130] established by the ICC, the victim's procedural rights shall be the primordial basis that the ICC should promote in benefit of victims. It has been unfortunately noticed that victim's participatory rights raise a problem of interpretation under the ICC. Both prosecution and defense have to face a proceedings challenge relating to "*views and concerns*"[131]before the Appeals Chamber with the aim of implying the involvement of victims regarding introduction of their evidence, and right of access to the prosecutor's documents.[132] Additionally, this underscores a problem of interference in the prosecutorial discretion and an equality of arms principle.[133] In clearer terms, this Court seems to defer the scope of Article 68(3) of Rome Statute in favor of the accused and in detriment to the interests of victims on the ground that their participation may be prejudicial to the rights of the accused.[134] But the question that appears, overall, in this thesis project focuses on the misconception of "the interests of justice" under the provisions of Article 53(1)(c) and (2)(c); and the absolute value of human dignity. Should the perpetrators sometimes escape from the Court's prosecution on the ground of any domestic amnesty? The response to this concern must radically and definitely be negative when we think about aftermaths of those gross violation of human rights.

---

[130] *See* Rome Statute, Art.68 (3).

[131] *See* No. ICC-01/04-01/07-1788-tENG, Trial Chamber II, 22 January 2010, ¶¶ 58-60.

[132] Situation in the Democratic Republic of the Congo, Case of Prosecutor v. Thomas Lubanga Dyilo, Judgement on the appeals of The Prosecutor and The Defence against Trial Chamber I's Decision on Victims' Participation of 18 January 2008, Case No. ICC-01/04-01/06-1432, 11 July 2008.

[133] On the wide prosecutorial discretion in international tribunals, *see* K. Howarth, Special Court for Sierra Leone – Fair Trials and Justice for the Accused 8 ICLR 399 at 403-409 (2008/3).

[134] *See supra* note 125; (Article 68(3) says that: "Where the personal interests of the victims are affected, the Court shall permit their views and concerns to be presented and considered at stages of the proceedings determined to be appropriate by the Court and in a manner which is not prejudicial to or inconsistent with the rights of the accused and a fair and impartial trial. Such views and concerns may be presented by the legal representatives of the victims where the Court considers it appropriate, in accordance with the Rules of Procedure and Evidence.").

A-Direct And Indirect Victims

This section examines the victims of gross violation of human rights and their family, as well as negative impacts on their future. Victims are any person, or civilian who does not belong to the conflict.[135]They are neither combatant nor fighter. They have the status of civilian. In other words, they are determined by their neutral character in the hostilities. Even as, in hostilities, the persons who are in resistance within population lay down their arms, they still maintain their civilian characteristic.[136] In fact, those persons or civilians are sometimes targeted, attacked, and/or killed either in war time or peace time. In other words, they are victim of genocide, crimes against humanity, war crimes, or crime of aggression.[137] Further, even though those persons died during the hostilities, or passed away after the hostilities they should always be regarded as victims on behalf of their community, as well as the global society. This not only for the deterrence; but also for the respect of human dignity. Because, in this context there are direct victims and indirect victims. First, direct victims individuals against whom a crime has been committed or attempted;[138]second indirect victims are those who have indirectly been victim of aftermaths such

[135] *See* Geneva or Hague Conventions, Art. 50 of AP I; *See* also *infra* note 176 at 313. ("Read together, Article 50 of Additional Protocol I and Article 4 A of the Third Geneva Convention establish that members of the armed forces, and members of militias or volunteer corps forming part of such armed forces, cannot claim civilian status. Neither can members of organized resistance groups, provided that they are commanded by a person responsible for his subordinates, that they have a fixed distinctive sign recognizable at a distance, that they carry arms openly, and that they conduct their operations in accordance with the laws and customs of war").

[136] *See* Prosecutor v. Blaškić, Case No. IT-95-14-A, Appeals Judgement ¶ 113 (Int'l Crim. Trb. For the Former Yugoslavia July 29, 2004).

[137] *See* Uganda situation where "they are gross human rights abuses **war crimes**, including murder; cruel treatment of civilians; intentionally directing an attack against a civilian population; pillaging; inducing rape; and forced enlistment of children; and **crimes against humanity**, including murder; enslavement; sexual enslavement; rape; and inhumane acts of inflicting serious bodily injury and suffering". *See* also situation in Darfur, Libya, Georgia, Bangladesh/Myanmar where they a lot of civilian's victim of gravest international crimes; available at www.icc-cpi.int/uganda/libya, etc. (so, do that make sense to grant amnesty to those perpetrators without investigation, or prosecution under alibi of ongoing peace process, or interests of justice? The response in this project is always NO, and will be it forever.).

[138] *See* Law Insider, Online dictionary available at https://www.lawinsider.com/dictionary.

as kids, family members, friends; without forgetting the psychosis traits and feelings that may stigmatize their ephemeral life.

B-Circumstantial Victims

Here, it is crucial to think about the child soldiers[139] who have been forced recruitment and are enlisted in the conflicts because of their social vulnerability. We might qualify them as circumstantial victims, on the ground of their will and age, despite that they also get involved in the commission of some crimes. Moreover, prisoners of war may also be regarded as circumstantial victims in armed conflict when they undergo a violation from the other party, with regard to the Third Geneva Convention, under the international humanitarian law.[140]

1-Circumstantial Victims: Child Soldiers

Human Rights Watch states: "[t]housands of children are serving as soldiers in armed conflicts around the world. They are boys and girls. Some as young as 8 years old, serve in government forces and armed opposition groups".[141] "They may fight on the front lines, participate in suicide missions, and act as spies, messengers, or lookouts. Girls may be forced into sexual slavery".[142]

---

[139] *See* Roos Haer, *Children and armed conflict: looking at the future and learning from the past*, Third World Quarterly, 40:1, 74-91, available at https://www.tandfonline.com/doi/full/ DOI: 10.1080/01436597.2018.1552131. (Accessed on October 3, 2020 at 6:32 P.M.).

The standard definition of a child soldier was formulated by the United Nations Children's Fund (UNICEF) in 2007; 'A "child soldier" is any child – boy or girl- under 18 years of age, who is part of any kind of regular or irregular armed force or armed group in any capacity, including, but not limited to cooks, porters, messengers, and anyone accompanying such groups other than family members.' This definition has been adopted in the Optional Protocol to the Convention on the Rights of the Child on the Involvement of Children in Armed Conflict, but also as international law in 2000. Before that, two of the most influential reports on children in conflict—the UN Machel Report of 1996 and the UN 1989 Convention on the Rights of the Child – also defined children as those under age of 18. I recognize, however, that this threshold is not without controversy. It is especially contested by anthropologists and sociologists working in childhood studies (see e.g., Hart, 'Saving Children'; and James and James, *Key Concepts*). It is additionally important to note that the term 'child soldiers' does not solely refer to children active as fighters. On the contrary, child soldiers have often supportive roles in an armed group. For instance, they are active as cooks, intelligence officers, carriers, etc."

[140] Geneva Convention III, Aug. (1949).

[141] *See* Human Rights Watch statement, available at https://www.hrw.org/topic/childrens-rights/child-soldiers. (It is important to outline that Human Rights Watch is a Non-Profit International Organization of human rights.).

[142] *Id.*

"Many are abducted or recruited by forces, while others join out of desperation, believing that armed groups offer their best chance for survival".[143] Non-State armed groups are responsible for most child recruitment around the world.[144] For instance, Iran continues to force or coerce children to fight with militias in Syria and funds militias using child soldiers in Iraq and Yemen.[145] Sometimes, young people cannot make a decision in whether or not they become members of the militia. Ross Haer asserts: "they have been represented as not having a free choice and thus as having been forcibly recruited, while adults in the same situation are generally assumed to have joined voluntarily and thus to have had a free choice".[146] This scholar attempts to support Wessells Richard[147] who argued that conflict times represent an opportunity for children to be used as child soldiers.[148]

Accordingly, the object of this project is to hold accountable the responsible persons that forced, or recruited children into armed conflict in taking advantage of their age, will and social vulnerability. These acts directed against children in the twenty first century world would constitute a destruction of the humanity; however, any child soldier would not be shielded from

---

[143] *Id.*

[144] *See* Jo Becker declaration, *Record Number of Countries on US Child Soldiers Blacklist*, ¶ 2 June 29, 2020 12:22PM EDT; available at https://www.hrw.org/news/2020/06/29/record-number-countries-us-child-soldier-blacklist (Last visited October 3, 2020 at 6:01 P.M.). Jo emphasized that:

> "[t]he Child Soldiers Prevention Act offers little leverage to influence child soldier use in countries like Syria or Iran, where the US provides no military assistance. And presidents have routinely used their waiver authority to continue military aid to countries still using child soldiers. Last year, for example, waivers allowed Afghanistan, Democratic Republic of Congo, Iraq, Mali, and Somalia to receive $17 million in military training and assistance.
>
> The State Department should use its diplomatic influence to press all countries on the list to end their involvement in child soldiering. The White House will not make its waiver decisions until September, but it should send a clear message: if you want US military aid, you can't use children as soldiers".

[145] *Id.*

[146] *See*, Roos Haer, *supra* note 139, at *94.

[147] Michael Wessells is an experienced child protection practitioner with Christian Children's Fund and Professor at Columbia University and Randolph-Macon College.

[148] *See*, Ross Haer, *supra* note 139.

impunity at age 18. They shall be held accountable for any international crime committed when they are no longer a child soldier.

2-Circumstantial Victims: Prisoner Of War

According to the international humanitarian law, a combatant who falls into the hands of an adverse party to a conflict in the course of an international armed conflict is a prisoner of war. They shall be treated with dignity.[149] Likewise, civilians who participate in the hostilities also benefit from guarantees of treatment in international and non-international armed conflicts.[150]However, the status of combatant is not officially recognized for members of Non-State armed groups in non-international armed conflicts. But, humanitarian law applicable to non-international armed conflicts provides a specific regime of protection for persons deprived of their liberty, under the status of detainee, for reasons related to the conflict. This status is often applied to Non-State armed groups members who fall into hands of their adversary. Those persons must also be humanely treated,[151] and shall not undergo "willful killing, torture or inhuman treatment, including biological experiments, willfully causing great suffering or serious injury to body or health, compelling a prisoner of war to serve in the forces of the hostile Power, or willfully depriving a prisoner of war of the rights of fair and regular trial prescribed in this Convention".[152]

---

149 *See* Geneva Convention, *supra* note 125, GCI–III.
150 *Id.* (GCI-V).
151 GCI–IV Common Art. 3, APII Art. 4.
152 GCIII Art. 130.

Indeed, those acts committed against these circumstantial victims shall not be left for amnesty without prior investigation on the facts. These are grave breaches of human rights that deserve to be investigated, prosecuted and punished under the international criminal law.

Conclusion

For the purpose of this project, this chapter outlines the scope of Article 53 of the Rome Statute towards a propulsion of the protection of victims, directly as well as indirectly. Furthermore, it upholds the protection of child soldiers regarded also as circumstantial victims because of their age, will, social vulnerability. They must always be protected even as we are aware of some of their acts in the commission of international crimes. This status of circumstantial victim should not be an excuse to shield them from impunity; but rather considered as an attenuation in the sentence with regard to the responsibility of their superior or recruiter. Therefore, the affirmative duty power of the prosecutor should be used for the interests of the justice in detriment to any alternative justice methods which do not represent to the real concept of justice. Otherwise, the memory and the vulnerability of victims have to be respected, and should not throw away in oblivion, under the provisions of Article 53 of the Rome Statute for any amnesty because of a misconception of the terms "interests of justice."

CHAPTER 4 : CRIMES[153] UNDER ICC[154] AND THEIR GAPS AGAINST THE VICTIM'S PROTECTION

The gross violation of human rights shall be punished and prosecuted. So, it is the duty of every State to exercise its legal obligation over those accountable for international crimes.[155]In case of those unwilling or unable to exercise their jurisdiction, the ICC can do it. It makes the unwilling or unable determination when required. Thus, the ICC has jurisdiction over genocide, crimes against humanity, war crimes, and the crime of aggression. It is important to highlight that with regard to international tribunals, the crime of aggression[156] is unique to the Rome Statute. Despite all these legal obligations, victims are confronted with the effective protection of their interests. That is to say, each of those core crimes exposes juridical gaps that put the victims within an incertitude of protection of their fundamental rights. With this perspective, this chapter attempts to emphasize those legal gaps and then gives an assumption of enforcement to most of core crimes falling into the ICC jurisdiction.

---

[153] Under the Rome Statute.

[154] Although the treaty of Rome Statute entered into force upon the 60 the ratification on July 1, 2002, 123 countries are now States Parties to the Rome Statute, the United States is not a party and only signed the Rome Statute at the end of President Clinton's second term on December 31, 2000, http://wwww.icc-cpi.int/Menus/ASP/states+parties. President Bush "unsigned" the treaty shortly thereafter in May 2002; on the ground that the ICC might politically be used against American service-members abroad, seen that there is no the constitutional right to a jury trial (the ICC uses a panel of judges). Hence, this perception prevented the Clinton, Bush, and Obama administrations from moving forward with the treaty.

[155] *Supra* note 2, (ICCSt. Preamble).

[156] The Rome Statute does not give the meaning of the crime of aggression. But the Review Conference at Kampala in June 2010 established a definition of the crime; and then in December 2017, the Assembly of State Parties adopted a resolution to activate the ICC's jurisdiction over the crime of aggression as of July 17, 2018.

I-Genocide

Although the crimes of genocide would be analyzed under the Rome Statute, it would be obvious to consider it *a priori* under the international tribunals ad hoc. For instance, the Nuremberg Tribunal classified them as a component of crimes against humanity. Emphasizing that the term "genocide" did not exist before. Viewing the quintessence of the nature of those crimes, Raphael Lemkin[157] created the term "genocide" that is accepted by the international community in 1948. According to him, there were no existing words that could sufficiently describe the horrors of the Holocaust.[158] Further, Winston Churchill linked those horrible crimes to the Nazis' large-scale exterminations as "*a crime without a name*".[159]Thus, Raphael made the construction of this term "from the ancient Greek word *genos* (race, tribe) and the Latin *cide* (killing) corresponding in its formations to such words as tyrannicide, homicide, infanticide, etc." Furthermore, towards an approach to punishment, this term was printed in the acceptation of the U.N. General Assembly that adopted the Convention on the Prevention and Punishment of the Crime of Genocide, classifying it as the most heinous international crimes.[160] Thus, it is defined as: "any of the following acts committed with intent to destroy, in whole or in part, a national, ethnical, racial or religious group [...]."[161]Furthermore, the convention mentions that the following acts of genocide

---

[157] Raphael Lemkin is a Polish scholar who immigrated to the United States in 1941.

[158] *See* Laurie R. Blank and Gregory P. Noone, INTERNATIONAL LAW AND ARMED CONFLICT, *Fundamental Principles and contemporary Challenges in the Law of War*, pp. 714-715 (2013).

[159] Katherine G. Southwick, *Srebrenica as Genocide? The Krstić Decision and the Language of the Unspeakable*, YALE HUMAN RIGHTS & DEVELOPMENT L.J. 08, at *227 (2005).

[160] *See* Convention on the Prevention and Punishment of the Crime of Genocide, adopted by U.N. General assembly (1948). Available at https://treaties.un.org/doc/publication/unts/volume%2078/volume-78-i-1021-english.pdf. (Accessed on Apr. 22, 2020 at 1:28 PM); also *see* Ivana Nizich, *International Law Weekend Proceedings: International Tribunals and Their Ability to Provide Adequate Justice: Lessons from The Yugoslav Tribunal*, 7 ILSA J Int'l & Comp L 353, at *354-*358 (2001).

[161] *Id.* Art. 2.

such as conspiracy, direct and public incitement, attempt, and complicity shall be punished.[162]Meaning genocide is prohibited in times of war as well as peace.

Moreover, under the Rome Statute of ICC "genocide"[163] means: "any of the following acts committed with intent to destroy, in whole or in part, a national, ethnical, racial or religious group, as such:

(a) Killing members of the group;

(b) Causing serious bodily or mental harm to members of the group;

(c) Deliberately inflicting on the group conditions of life calculated to bring about its physical destruction in whole or in part;

(d) Imposing measures intended to prevent births within the group;

(e) Forcibly transferring children of the group to another group."

It shall be noted that the Convention's definition of "genocide" has been verbatim exported in the Rome Statute; as well as the Statutes of international Tribunals. So, in comparative observation, it is obvious to highlight that its target character, to "intent" towards a "group", is the fundamental element of differentiation in war crimes from crimes against humanity. Hence, considering the term "genocide" through its meaning (as defined by Raphael Lemkin), it might seem that the crimes of genocide are, nowadays, trading away from its real nature. In other words, as emphasized by it Laurie R. Blank and Gregory P. Noone, is this term in perfect intrinsic adequacy with the real nature of meaning of crimes? Or if "*Geno*" means race from Greek, is it sufficient to assert that "race" necessarily means "group"? Or are the commission of those crimes

---

[162] *Id.* Art. 3.

[163] *See* Rome Statute, Art.6.

only limited on race? Those interrogations require a deep analysis in order to protect the victims from any juridical void.[164] In fact, this analysis of classification of crimes of genocide enables us towards the identification of new international crimes named "groupicide." The construction of this crime follows the neological step of Raphael Lemkin. That is to say, it is based on two words, ***groupe*** from French meaning group and then ***cide*** from Latin meaning killed. So the paramount question here focuses on the legal definition of the word "Group".

A-Meaning of Groupicide

In accordance with the principles proclaimed in the Charter of the United Nations[165], recognition of the inherent dignity and of the equal and inalienable rights of all members of the human family is the foundation of freedom, justice and peace in the world.

The people of the United Nations, in the Charter, reaffirm their faith in fundamental human rights and in the dignity and worth of the human person and are determined to protect human beings and promote larger fundamental freedoms.

Recognizing that the United Nations has, in the Universal Declaration of Human Rights[166] and in the International Covenants on Human Rights, proclaims and agrees that everyone is entitled to all the rights and freedoms set forth therein, without distinction of any kind, such as race, colour, sex, language, religion, political or opinion, national or social origin, property, birth or other status. Recalling that, in the Universal Declaration of Human Rights, the United Nations proclaims that

---

164 *Supra* note 158, p.722; Prosecutor v. Krstić, Case No. IT-98-33-A, Judgement ¶ 36-37 (Int'l Crim. Trib. For the Former Yugoslavia, April 19, 2004), ["The Appeals Chamber states unequivocally that the law condemns, **in appropriate terms**, the deep and lasting injury inflicted, and calls the massacre at Srebrenica by its proper name: genocide. Those responsible will bear this stigma, and it will serve a warning to those who may in future contemplate the commission of such a heinous act"].

165 U.N. Charter, available at https://www.treaties.un.org/doc/publication/ctc/uncharter.pdf.

166 Universal Declaration of Human Rights, Adopted 10 December 1948, GA Res. 217 A (III).

all human beings are born free and equal in dignity and rights. They are endowed with reason and conscience and should act towards one another in a spirit of brotherhood.

Recognizing that the human beings living in society as fundamental diverse groups of society and the natural environment living in society should be afforded the necessary protection so that they can fully assume their responsibilities within the community.

Recognizing that all human beings, for the full and harmonious development of his or her personality, should live in peace and security in a family, in a group, in an environment, in an atmosphere of happiness, love and understanding regardless their opinion, or political, association, cultural, religious, affiliation or membership.

Recognizing that persons are targeted, destroyed, or deprived of their liberty because of their group affiliation or membership for decades. Considering that human beings should, but don't always, feel fully comfortable to live an individual life in society; thus, it is important to live with the spirit of the ideals proclaimed in the Charter of the United Nations, and in particular in the spirit of peace, dignity, tolerance, freedom, equality and solidarity.

Bearing in mind that the need to extend particular protection to the persons living in group according to the nature of their membership, or affiliation, has been recognized in the Universal Declaration of Human Rights, in the International Covenant on Civil and Political Rights[167] (in particular in Articles 1, 5 and 18), in the International Covenant on Economic, Social and Cultural Rights[168] (in particular in Article 1 and 2) and in the statutes and relevant instruments of specialized

---

[167] International Covenant on Civil and Political Rights (ICCPR), adopted 16 December 1966, GA Res. 2200A (XXI), 999 UNTS 171.

[168] International Covenant on Economic, Social and Cultural Rights (CESCR), adopted 16 December 1966, GA Res. 2200A (XXI), UN Doc. A/6316 (1966), 993 UNTS 3.

agencies and international organizations concerned with the protection of fundamental freedom rights,[169] those people need protection under the classification of crimes of groupicide.

Convinced that the protection of persons targeted, destroyed, or deprived of their liberty against the nature of their group affiliation, or membership such as: social, cultural, religious, philosophy, political, shall be strengthened by the importance of international cooperation.

Hereby this thesis attempts to argue, that *groupicide*, whether committed in time of peace or in time of war, is a crime under international law which the international community must undertake to prevent and punish. This thesis's goal is to enforce the genocide convention created by Raphael and refine it in order to fill the gap.

B-Legal Definition Of Group

A group means a certain number of people, belonging to a specific community, or association, sharing the same values, philosophies, or ideologies, except the Non-State actors or members of criminal enterprises, with regard to their socio-cultural, religious, association, political affiliation, or membership. Moreover, the status of groups shall be determined with regard to a reasonable and sufficient number of affiliation or membership.

[169] Convention for the Protection of Human Rights and Fundamental Freedoms (ECHR), adopted 4 November 1950, ETS 5, 213 UNTS 221; International Convention on the Elimination of All Forms of Racial Discrimination (CERD), adopted 21 December 1965, GA Res. 2106 (XX), annex, UN Doc. A/6014 (1966), 660 UNTS 195; American Convention on Human Rights (ACHR), adopted 22 November 1969, OAS Treaty Ser. No. 36, 1144 UNTS 123; African Charter on Human and Peoples' Rights (AChHR), adopted 27 June 1981, OAU Doc. CAB/LEG/67/3 rev. 5, 1520 UNTS 217, etc.

For the purpose of this project, groupicide means any of the following acts committed with intent to destroy, in whole or in part, a group or association, sharing political, religious, philosophic, or cultural ideas such as:

(a) Killing members of the group;

(b) Causing serious bodily or mental harm to members of the group;

(c) Deliberately inflicting on the group conditions of life calculated to bring about its physical destruction in whole or in part;

(d) Imposing measures intended to prevent births within the group;

(e) Forcibly transferring children of the group to another group;

(f) Causing serious prejudice on the group to prevent it from surviving socio-economically;

(g) Voting laws in the objective of preventing the members, or group from surviving politically, socially, or economically.

The following acts shall be punishable:

(a) Groupicide;

(b) Conspiracy to commit groupicide;

(c) Direct and public incitement to commit groupicide;

(d) Attempt to commit groupicide;

(e) Complicity in groupicide.

Persons committing groupicide, groupicidal acts, or any of the other acts enumerated above shall be punished, whether they are constitutionally responsible rulers, public officials or private individuals. States shall take all appropriate measures to ensure that the groups are protected against all forms of discrimination or punishment on the basis of their status, activities, expressed opinions, or beliefs of their members. In other words, some people are targeted because of their religion, culture, opinion, associative membership, sex, or disability status and crimes stemming from these believes shall not be considered as political crimes. The philosophy behind this proposal's approach is, at the root, to demystify the myth of classification around word *Geno* in order to extend protection of human dignity towards diverse groups of the global community who are targeted against their affiliation, or membership by the political leaders.[170]

II-Crimes Against Humanity

Crimes against humanity are also crimes related to international concern. Prior to ICC existence, crimes against humanity seem to be confused to war crimes. Indeed, General Telford Taylor, defined them as: "These crimes cover the vast and terrible world of the Nuremberg laws, yellow arm bands, "aryanization", concentration camps, medical experiments, extermination squads, and so on..." Actually, "when committed in the course of belligerent occupation" (whether in the occupied country or elsewhere), these were also "war crimes". But the concept of crimes against humanity comprises atrocities which are part of a campaign of discrimination or persecution, and which are crimes against international law even when committed by nationals of one country against their fellow nationals or against those of other nations irrespective of

[170] In Benin, like many other countries in the world, many people are targeted, constraint to aisle, even killed because of their political opinion. (For instance, under the government of President Patrice Talon, all the members of the opposition, as well persons who have different opinion against his power are targeted, and assassinated, imprisoned, or constraint to aisle). Note that Patrice Talon has been democratically, elected in 2016 as Benin's President. Moreover, some people are also target because of their sexual orientation, of fact that they belong to LGBTQ community. The white supremacy in the USA could also be regarded as act of groupicide exercised against the minorities with black or brown skin. This conducted to an assault to the Capitol, the breath of the American democracy on January 6, 2020. Many scholars considered that act as domestic terrorism.

belligerent status.[171] However, highlighting that acts of crimes against humanity are technically be different of war crimes. This has been acknowledged under the Rome Statute. Specifically, "[f]or the purpose of this Statute, "crime against humanity"[172] means any of the following acts when committed as part of a widespread or systematic attack directed against **any civilian population,** with knowledge of the attack":

(a) "Murder;

(b) Extermination;

(c) Enslavement;

(d) Deportation or forcible transfer of population;

(e) Imprisonment or other severe deprivation of physical liberty in violation of fundamental rules of international law;

(f) Torture;

(g) Rape, sexual slavery, enforced prostitution, forced pregnancy, enforced sterilization, or any other form of sexual violence of comparable gravity;

(h) Persecution against any identifiable group or collectivity on political, racial, national, ethnic, cultural, religious, gender as defined in paragraph 3, or other grounds that are universally recognized as impermissible under international law,

---

[171] Telford Taylor, *Final Report to the Secretary of the Army on the Nuremberg War Crimes Trials under control Council Law*, No. 10 64-65 (1949). Recall that General Telford Taylor was Chief Prosecutor for the Nuremberg Subsequent Proceedings.

[172] *See* Rome Statute, Art.7.

in connection with any act referred to in this paragraph or any crime within the jurisdiction of the Court;

(i) Enforced disappearance of persons;

(j) The crime of apartheid;

(k) Other inhumane acts of a similar character intentionally causing great suffering, or serious injury to body or to mental or physical health".

For the purpose of paragraph 1:

(a) "Attack directed against any civilian population" means a course of conduct involving the multiple commission of acts referred to in paragraph 1 against any civilian population, pursuant to or in furtherance of a State or organizational policy to commit such attack;

(b) "Extermination" includes the intentional infliction of conditions of life, *inter alia* the deprivation of access to food and medicine, calculated to bring about the destruction of part of a population;

(c) "Enslavement" means the exercise of any or all of the powers attaching to the right of ownership over a person and includes the exercise of such power in the course of trafficking in persons, in particular women and children;

(d) "Deportation or forcible transfer of population" means forced displacement of the persons concerned by expulsion or other coercive acts from the area in which they are lawfully present, without grounds permitted under international law;

(e) "Torture" means the intentional infliction of severe pain or suffering, whether physical or mental, upon a person in the custody or under the control of the accused; except that torture shall not include pain or suffering arising only from, inherent in or incidental to, lawful sanctions;

(f) "Forced pregnancy" means the unlawful confinement of a woman forcibly made pregnant, with the intent of affecting the ethnic composition of any population or carrying out other grave violations of international law. This definition shall not in any way be interpreted as affecting national laws relating to pregnancy;

(g) "Persecution" means the intentional and severe deprivation of fundamental rights contrary to international law by reason of the identity of the group or collectivity;

(h) "The crime of apartheid" means inhumane acts of a character similar to those referred to in paragraph 1, committed in the context of an institutionalized regime of systematic oppression and domination by one racial group over any other racial group or groups and committed with the intention of maintaining that regime.

In fact, the fundamental elements required in light of this definition for identifying a crime against humanity are based on requirements of "an attack" which must be "widespread or systematic"; and then "must be directed against any civilian population." Apart from those, the acts of the accused must be part of the attack; and then he or she had to be aware of the commission of a "widespread or systematic attack." But, the main question about this definition is when a crime against humanity occurred in armed conflict, is there no protection for those victims? Or would the protection of victims be limited in case of crimes against humanity? Given that an attack could be directed against one or any person, should we assert that "civilian" means "Civilian population"? Or what do the terms "Civilian population" mean in paragraph 2 (a)?[173]. ICC has competence to exercise its jurisdiction in peacetime as well as wartime contrarily to the ad hoc International Criminal Tribunals. Regarding this topic, Professor Leila Nadya Sadat says: "[t]he civilian population comprises all persons who are civilians."[174] Absolutely! But the crucial question in this thesis is to touch the quintessence of that definition. Because this term was borrowed from the Statute of Ad hoc International Criminal Tribunals which exercised their competence only in wartime. The definition cannot be deemed complete. In other words, this meaning of civilian population was addressed under the international humanitarian law that is just a part of international criminal law. However, should civilian population mean civilian in peacetime? This thesis attempts to weight the definition of "civilian population" to civilian with regard to human dignity. The word "population" undoubtedly is emphasizing the number or amount of civilians unlike the term "civilian".

III- War Crimes

Unlike other international legal instruments, the meaning of war crime is[175] broadly detailed under the ICC. In other words, it is observed differently in international armed conflict[176]on the

---

[173] *Id.*

[174] *See* Leila Nadya Sadat *Putting Peacetime First: Crimes Against Humanity And The Civilian Population Requirement*, 31 Emory Int'l L. Rev. 197, at *217 (2017).

[175] Rome Statute, Art.8.

[176] John B. Bellinger III and Vijay M. Padmanabhan, Detention Operations In Contemporary Conflicts*: Four Challenges For The Geneva Conventions And Other Existing Law*, 105 A.J.I.L. 201, 201, at *204 (2011).

first hand, and in non-international armed conflict on the second hand[177]. It is considered firstly as a grave breach of the four Geneva Conventions:

(i) Wilful killing;

(ii) Torture or inhuman treatment, including biological experiments;

(iii) Wilfully causing great suffering, or serious injury to body or health;

(iv) Extensive destruction and appropriation of property, not justified by military necessity and carried out unlawfully and wantonly;

(v) Compelling a prisoner of war or other protected person to serve in the forces of a hostile Power;

(vi) Wilfully depriving a prisoner of war or other protected person of the rights of fair and regular trial;

(vii) Unlawful deportation or transfer or unlawful confinement;

(viii) Taking of hostages.

Additionally, the Rome Statute describes twenty-six war crimes as: "[o]ther serious violations of the laws and customs applicable in international armed conflict, within the established framework of international law, namely, any of the following acts:

(i) Intentionally directing attacks against the civilian population as such or against individual civilians not taking direct part in hostilities;

(ii) Intentionally directing attacks against civilian objects, that is, objects which are not military objectives;

---

[177] *Id.* at *205.

(iii) Intentionally directing attacks against personnel, installations, material, units or vehicles involved in a humanitarian assistance or peacekeeping mission in accordance with the Charter of the United Nations, as long as they are entitled to the protection given to civilians or civilian objects under the international law of armed conflict;

(iv) Intentionally launching an attack in the knowledge that such attack will cause incidental loss of life or injury to civilians or damage to civilian objects or widespread, long-term and severe damage to the natural environment which would be clearly excessive in relation to the concrete and direct overall military advantage anticipated;

(v) Attacking or bombarding, by whatever means, towns, villages, dwellings or buildings which are undefended and which are not military objectives;

(vi) Killing or wounding a combatant who, having laid down his arms or having no longer means of defense, has surrendered at discretion;

(vii) Making improper use of a flag of truce, of the flag or of the military insignia and uniform of the enemy or of the United Nations, as well as of the distinctive emblems of the Geneva Conventions, resulting in death or serious personal injury;

(viii) The transfer, directly or indirectly, by the Occupying Power of parts of its own civilian population into the territory it occupies, or the deportation or transfer of all or parts of the population of the occupied territory within or outside this territory;

(ix) Intentionally directing attacks against buildings dedicated to religion, education, art, science or charitable purposes, historic monuments, hospitals and places where the sick and wounded are collected, provided they are not military objectives;

(x) Subjecting persons who are in the power of an adverse party to physical mutilation or to medical or scientific experiments of any kind which are neither justified by the medical, dental or hospital treatment of the person concerned nor carried out in his or her interest, and which cause death to or seriously endanger the health of such person or persons;

(xi) Killing or wounding treacherously individuals belonging to the hostile nation or army;

(xii) Declaring that no quarter will be given;

(xiii) Destroying or seizing the enemy's property unless such destruction or seizure be imperatively demanded by the necessities of war;

(xiv) Declaring abolished, suspended or inadmissible in a court of law the rights and actions of the nationals of the hostile party;

(xv) Compelling the nationals of the hostile party to take part in the operations of war directed against their own country, even if they were in the belligerent's service before the commencement of the war;

(xvi) Pillaging a town or place, even when taken by assault;

(xvii) Employing poison or poisoned weapons;

(xviii) Employing asphyxiating, poisonous or other gases, and all analogous liquids, materials or devices;

(xix) Employing bullets which expand or flatten easily in the human body, such as bullets with a hard envelope which does not entirely cover the core or is pierced with incisions;

(xx) Employing weapons, projectiles and material and methods of warfare which are of a nature to cause superfluous injury or unnecessary suffering or which are inherently indiscriminate in violation of the international law of armed conflict, provided that such weapons, projectiles and material and methods of warfare are the subject of comprehensive prohibition and are included in an annex to this Statute, by an amendment in accordance with the relevant provisions set forth in articles 121 and 123;

(xxi) Committing outrages upon personal dignity, in particular humiliating and degrading treatment;

(xxii) Committing rape, sexual slavery, enforced prostitution, forced pregnancy, as defined in article 7, paragraph 2 (f), enforced sterilization, or any other form of sexual violence also constituting a grave breach of the Geneva Conventions;

(xxiii) Utilizing the presence of a civilian or other protected person to render certain points, areas or military forces immune from military operations;

(xxiv) Intentionally directing attacks against buildings, material, medical units and transport, and personnel using the distinctive emblems of the Geneva Conventions in conformity with international law;

(xxv) Intentionally using starvation of civilians as a method of warfare by depriving them of objects indispensable to their survival, including Wilfully impeding relief supplies as provided for under the Geneva Conventions;

(xxvi) Conscripting or enlisting children under the age of fifteen years into the national armed forces or using them to participate actively in hostilities.

In the case of an armed conflict without international character, serious violations of Article 3[178] common to the four Geneva Conventions of 12 August 1949, namely, any of the following acts committed against persons taking no active part in the hostilities, including members of armed forces who have laid down their arms and those placed hors de combat by sickness, wounds, detention or any other cause:

(i) Violence to life and person, in particular murder of all kinds, mutilation, cruel treatment and torture;

---

[178] *See* David A. Elder, *The Historical Background of Common Article 3 of the Geneva Convention of 1949*, 11 Case W. Res. J. Int'l L. 37 (1979) ["The laws of war are] based on certain of the fundamental rights proclaimed in it [Declaration] -respect for the human person, protection against torture and against cruel, inhuman or degrading punishments or treatment. Those rights find their legal expression in the contractual engagements which your Governments have today agreed to undertake "].

Recalling that ARTICLE 3 is common to the four Geneva Conventions of 1949: "In the case of armed conflict not of an international character occurring in the territory of one of the High Contracting Parties, each Party to the conflict shall be bound to apply, as a minimum, the following provisions:

(1) Persons taking no active part in the hostilities, including members of armed forces who have laid down their arms and those placed ' hors de combat ' by sickness, wounds, detention, or any other cause, shall in all circumstances be treated humanely, without any adverse distinction founded on race, colour, religion or faith, sex, birth or wealth, or any other similar criteria. To this end, the following acts are and shall remain prohibited at any time and in any place whatsoever with respect to the above-mentioned persons: (a) violence to life and person, in particular murder of all kinds, mutilation, cruel treatment and torture; (b) taking of hostages; (c) outrages upon personal dignity, in particular humiliating and degrading treatment; (d) the passing of sentences and the carrying out of executions without previous judgment pronounced by a regularly constituted court, affording all the judicial guarantees which are recognized as indispensable by civilized peoples.

(2) The wounded and sick shall be collected and cared for. An impartial humanitarian body, such as the International Committee of the Red Cross, may offer its services to the Parties to the conflict. The Parties to the conflict should further endeavour to bring into force, by means of special agreements, all or part of the other provisions of the present Convention. The application of the preceding provisions shall not affect the legal status of the Parties to the conflict." Available at http://www.adh-geneve.ch/RULAC/pdf/Common-Article-3.pdf; or also at http://www.crc.org/en/doc/assets/files/publications/icrc-002-0173.pdf. (Both accessed on Apr. 20, 2020 at 10:55 PM).

(ii) Committing outrages upon personal dignity, in particular humiliating and degrading treatment;

(iii) Taking of hostages;

(iv) The passing of sentences and the carrying out of executions without previous judgement pronounced by a regularly constituted court, affording all judicial guarantees which are generally recognized as indispensable.

Additionally, of war crimes listed in Article 8(2)(b) and 8(2)(c) which is applied to non-international armed conflicts and "thus, does not apply to situations of internal disturbances and tensions, such as riots, isolated and sporadic acts of violence or other acts of a similar nature," the Rome Statute provided in Article 8(2) (e) an approximatively identical list of "[o]ther serious violations of the laws and customs applicable in armed conflicts not of an international character, within the established framework of international law, namely, any of the following acts:[179]

(i) Intentionally directing attacks against the civilian population as such or against individual civilians not taking direct part in hostilities;

(ii) Intentionally directing attacks against buildings, material, medical units and transport, and personnel using the distinctive emblems of the Geneva Conventions in conformity with international law;

---

[179] *See* ICCSt. Art. 8(e) (2). (This paragraph applies to armed conflicts not of an international character and thus does not apply to situations of internal disturbances and tensions, such as riots, isolated and sporadic acts of violence or other acts of a similar nature. It applies to armed conflicts that take place in the territory of a State when there is protracted armed conflict between governmental authorities and organized armed groups or between such groups).

(iii) Intentionally directing attacks against personnel, installations, material, units or vehicles involved in a humanitarian assistance or peacekeeping mission in accordance with the Charter of the United Nations, as long as they are entitled to the protection given to civilians or civilian objects under the international law of armed conflict;

(iv) Intentionally directing attacks against buildings dedicated to religion, education, art, science or charitable purposes, historic monuments, hospitals and places where the sick and wounded are collected, provided they are not military objectives;

(v) Pillaging a town or place, even when taken by assault;

(vi) Committing rape, sexual slavery, enforced prostitution, forced pregnancy, as defined in article 7, paragraph 2 (f), enforced sterilization, and any other form of sexual violence also constituting a serious violation of article 3 common to the four Geneva Conventions;

(vii) Conscripting or enlisting children under the age of fifteen years into armed forces or groups or using them to participate actively in hostilities;

(viii) Ordering the displacement of the civilian population for reasons related to the conflict, unless the security of the civilians involved or imperative military reasons so demand;

(ix) Killing or wounding treacherously a combatant adversary;

(x) Declaring that no quarter will be given;

(xi) Subjecting persons who are in the power of another party to the conflict to physical mutilation or to medical or scientific experiments of any kind which are neither justified by the medical, dental or hospital treatment of the person concerned nor carried out in his or her interest, and which cause death to or seriously endanger the health of such person or persons;

(xii) Destroying or seizing the property of an adversary.

In comparing the different paragraphs of Article 8 of ICCSt.[180], we denote that the terms: <<Grave breach>> and <<Serious crimes>> deserve a necessary attention. They seem to influence the classification of crimes[181]by opening a door of evasion to criminals. In this regard, we shall mention that the right to protect the victims is non-negotiable. Otherwise, should the protection of victims depend on the context and crime retained? Or does this mean, under the international humanitarian law, that the States have an obligation to protect a person's dignity more so in international armed conflict than in non-international armed conflicts? Or were the victims protected under one or more of the Geneva Conventions, including Common Article? The response to these questions requires intense thought. War crimes, in international armed conflicts as well as in non-international armed conflicts, are perceived essentially under two angles: protection of persons and objects and conduct relating to breaches of important values (, such as desecration of the dead, humiliating treatment, or recruitment of child soldiers).[182] Indeed, crimes against protected persons constitute grave breaches under the four Geneva Conventions. In other words, the four Geneva Conventions lay down the notion of grave breaches only in protected person's

---

[180] *Id.* Art.8. (Nothing in paragraph 2 (c) and (e) shall affect the responsibility of a Government to maintain or re-establish law and order in the State or to defend the unity and territorial integrity of the State, by all legitimate means.).

[181] Wilful killing and Murder.

[182] Jean-Marie Henckaerts & Louise Doswald-Beck, 1 CUSTOMARY INTERNATIONAL HUMANITARIAN LAW, 569-570 (2005).

international armed conflict; respectively, in Articles 50,[183] 51,[184] 130[185] and 147.[186] It is, additionally, noticed that grave breaches provisions in Additional Protocol I includes additional grave breaches regarding treatment of persons.[187] Thus, the meaning of serious crimes are the crimes not mentioned in the provisions above such as the crimes directed against circumstantial victims; for instance, the enlistment and use of child soldiers in hostilities. There is a distortion under the international humanitarian law, despite the existence of common Article 3, concerning the protection of victims. The criminal responsibility seems to be less considered with regard to grave breaches and serious crimes. Moreover, some jurisprudence attempt to shift the confusion that those terms raises when aiming to protect the victims.[188]The violations of the laws and customs of war are considered serious if they endanger protected persons or objects or they breach important values; but when those violations are made wilfully, then it is question of grave breaches. In this regard, the term *grave breaches* will be tied to the principle of "mens rea". Meaning the

---

[183] GC-I, Art. 50. ("Grave breaches meaning ... shall be those involving any of the following acts, if committed against persons or property protected by the Convention: wilful killing, torture or inhuman treatment, including biological experiments, wilfully causing great suffering or serious injury to body or health, and extensive destruction and appropriation of property, not justified by military necessity and carried out unlawfully and wantonly").

[184]GC-II, Art. 51. ("Grave breaches... shall be those involving any of the following acts, if committed against persons or property protected by the Convention: wilful killing, torture or inhuman treatment, including biological experiments, wilfully causing great suffering or serious injury to body or health, and extensive destruction and appropriation of property, not justified by military necessity and carried out unlawfully and wantonly").

[185] GC-III Art. 130. ("Grave breaches... shall be those involving any of the following acts, if committed against persons or property protected by the Convention: wilful killing, torture or inhuman treatment, including biological experiments, wilfully causing great suffering or serious injury to body or health, compelling a prisoner of war to serve in the forces of the hostile Power, or wilfully depriving a prisoner of war of the rights of fair and regular trial prescribed in this Convention").

[186] GC-IV, Art. 147. ("Grave breaches ...shall be those involving any of the following acts, if committed against persons or property protected by the present Convention: wilful killing, torture or inhuman treatment, including biological experiments, wilfully causing great suffering or serious injury to body or health, unlawful deportation or transfer or unlawful confinement of a protected person, compelling a protected person to serve in the forces a hostile Power, or wilfully depriving a protected person of the rights of fair and regular trial prescribed in the present Convention, taking of hostages and extensive destruction and appropriation of property, not justified by military necessity and carried out unlawfully and wantonly").

[187] *See* Article 11 of Additional Protocol I includes "additional grave breaches regarding treatment of persons".

[188] *See* Tadić (Decision on Interlocutory Appeal on Jurisdiction), [ICTY Appeals Chamber] ¶ 94 ("the violation must be "serious", that is to say, it must constitute a breach of a rule protecting important values, and the breach must involve grave consequences for the victim").

term *serious* should be the "actus reus" of crime, and the grave breaches the "mens rea" of crime. The sum of both would be regarded as the **most** serious international crimes under the ICC, even in non-international armed conflict.

IV-Crimes Of Aggression

In New York in 2017, State Parties to the Rome Statute made the historic decision to enable the ICC to prosecute the crime of aggression regarding the Kampala amendments of 2010 with the authority to hold accountable those responsible committing for illegal use of force.[189] The effect of jurisdiction of the ICC over crime of aggression went into effect on 17 July 2018, which also marked the 20th anniversary of the Rome Statute.[190] Indeed, the legal meaning of use of force under the ICC belongs to the jurisprudence of International Court of Justice (ICJ).[191]The definition of act of aggression depicts the illegal use of force, namely those that manifestly violate the UN Charter by their «character, gravity and scale. » In this regard, the ICC involves the responsibility of Sates, and then the exclusion of Non-State actors in the commission of crimes of aggression.

Indeed, ICC was established with the aim to have jurisdiction over natural persons identified to have committed crimes that fall within the jurisdiction of this Court. Those core crimes such as the crimes against humanity, genocide, and war crimes, have dual obligations under the ICC.[192]The State concerned shall prosecute or extradite the perpetrators under the principle of complementarity. This means that the crimes under the Rome Statute are confined with a customary *erga omnes*, obligation upon States, and *aut dedere aut judicare* requiring to prosecute

[189] *See* icc-cpi.int.
[190] *Id.*
[191] *See Nicaragua v. United States (1986).*
[192] *See* Dapo Akande & Antonios Tzanakopoulos, *The Crime of Aggression in the ICC and State Responsibility*, 58, Harvard J. Int'l L. 32, Spring (2017).

or extradite.[193]However, there is no provision under the Rome Statute relating to the individual criminal responsibility that shall affect the responsibility of State under the international law even in goal of deterrence.[194]

Crime of aggression, as defined in the Rome Statute, seems to be limited to those individuals who exercise control over State.[195] The quintessence of the definition of crime of aggression under the Rome Statute exposes the " act of aggression" as a crime committed against the sovereignty of States; States and their citizens are confronted today by the attacks of armed group from Non-State actors in the global world.[196] Undoubtedly, these Non-State actors constitute an eminent threat for the sovereignty of States or are prejudicial to the territorial integrity of States concerned.[197]

So, crime of aggression under the Rome Statute should focus on the Non-State actors, criminal corporations, or enterprises rather than only on the officials who exercise control over a State. Further, the International Criminal Court does, unfortunately, not give the legal definition

---

193 *See* Diane Orentlicher, *supra* note 68, at* 2537.

194 Rome Statute, Art. 25(4).

195 *Id.* art. 8 bis (1).

196 *See* MacKennan Graziano and Lan Mei, 58, *The Crime of Aggression under the Rome Statute and Implications for Corporate Accountability*, 58 Harvard J. Int'l L. 60, Spring (2017).

197 *See* Michael P. Scharf, *How the War Against ISIS Changed International Law,* 48 Case W. Res. J. Int'l L. 60-61 (2016). M.P. Scharf affirmed:

> "[b]oth al-Qaeda and ISIS are widely viewed as representing a new kind of threat, in which a non-state actor possesses many of the attributes of a State: massive wealth, sophisticated training and organization, and access to destructive weaponry. To respond to the fundamental change presented by these uber-terrorist groups, the United States has argued that it is now lawful to attack such non-state actors when they are present in States that are unable or unwilling to curb them. In light of the Security Council approval of the 2001 invasion of Afghanistan to dislodge al-Qaeda and the absence of significant protest of the subsequent drone strikes against al-Qaeda leaders and operatives in Pakistan, Somalia, Iraq, and Yemen, international law seemed to be moving rapidly toward adoption of the "unable and unwilling" principle of self-defense. But in the 2004 Wall and 2005 Congo cases, the International Court of Justice reaffirmed that international law permits extraterritorial attacks against non-state actors only when their actions are attributable to the territorial state, utilizing an effective control standard. Despite widespread criticism of these holdings, including from some of the ICJ's most respected members, these judicial decisions unquestionably set back the evolving customary international law of self-defense against non-state actors".

of the expression " effective control over State" in order to avoid any confusion on the quintessence of Article 25(3) *bis*.[198] However, it may be accepted that the Court involves State responsibility by exercising its jurisdiction over the officials or agents of State concern. In this context, the debate on "natural person" and "legal person" would be raised. In other words, there is a principle of discrimination in the prosecution of crime of aggression under ICC where the Court may not exercise jurisdiction over Non-party States to the Rome Statute[199] whenever a crime of aggression is committed by a national of this Non-party States or on its territory. This means that Non-party States are excluded in this context, i.e. potential aggressor and victim States. This seems to be in contrast with Article 12(2), which otherwise protects the territory of State Parties in regard to genocide, crimes against humanity, and war crimes committed by nationals of Non-party States.[200] Similar with Article 12(3)[201] which permits Non-party States to accept the jurisdiction of the Court on ad hoc and case by case basis.

Thus, with regard to Article 5[202] and the provisions of Articles 12(2)[203] and 15(5)[204] expose an antagonism outlining the notion of discrimination regarding investigation and prosecution of crime of aggression under the Rome Statute of ICC. It is regrettable that the definition of crime of aggression and its prosecution is substantially incompatible with the provisions of Articles 12, 15 and 25 of the Rome Statute of the International Criminal Court.

---

[198] See Antonio Cassese, *The Nicaragua and Tadić Tests Revisited in Light of the ICJ Judgment on Genocide in Bosnia*, 18 Eur. J. Int'l. L. 649, 651–667 (2007) (commenting ICJ Case Concerning Military and Paramilitary Activities in and Against Nicaragua (Merits), judgment of 27 June 1986), available at http://www.ejil.org/pdfs/18/4/233.pdf (Accessed on Sept. 25, 2020).

[199] Rome Statute, Art. 15 bis (5).

[200] *Id.* art 12(2).

[201] *Id.* art 12(3).

[202] *Id.*

[203] *Id.*

[204] *Id.*

Conclusion

Undoubtedly, it is noticed that the core crimes in the Rome Statute of International Criminal Court exhibit quite large gaps that are in contrast with the respect of human rights. This disadvantages the interests of victims and sometimes may be deleterious to the integrity and fairness of trials under ICC. However, this thesis attempts to wake up the international conscience on the prejudices of those gaps and then proposes a legal framework for a substantial enforcement of the convention of genocide in light of an identification of new classification called <<*groupicide*>>. Further, this thesis attempts to draft a proposal of the Convention for its Prevention and Punishment.

PART III- THE RULE OF LAW UNDER INTERNATIONAL CRIMINAL COURT

CHAPTER 5: PROSECUTING UNDER ART.53, NARROWING TO THE VIENNA CONVENTION

This part of this project tackles the quintessence of Article 53 of ICCSt. It depicts the necessity to "initiate an investigation" and "decide to prosecute" on the ground of reasonable basis. In other words, the investigation, as well as prosecution, must base itself on some key factors according to the type of crimes which are obligatory for the protection of victims.

I-Obligation To Prosecute

As shown above, the proceedings of investigation and prosecution under the ICC still raise a lot of issues in detriment to victims. Indeed, the alternative justice methods, or national peace process constitute an enormous handicap in the balance of the notion of justice. Article 53 that is the discretionary power of the prosecutor, and which deserves to be the victims' voice necessities a strict substantial analysis in the commission of each type of the most serious international crimes.[205]It also emphasizes the boundaries that prosecutorial discretion face with some Non-party States to ICCSt. For instance, it is recently noted, that a full investigation and prosecution into alleged war crimes in Afghanistan, which would include an alleged crime committed by US

[205] For instance, in Afghanistan situation the Pre-Trial Chamber II decided that an investigation into the situation in Afghanistan at this stage would not serve the interests of justice, and accordingly, rejected the request of the OTP. available at https://www.icc-cpi.int/Pages/record.aspx?docNo=ICC-02/17-33. But the Appeals Chamber reversed the Pre-Trial Chamber II decision on March 5, 2020 and authorized the opening of the Afghanistan investigation. It held that:" There is no reason to limit the Prosecutor's investigation in the manner envisaged by the Pre-Trial Chamber". This is a strong signal for "the interests of justice". *See* Appeals Chamber judgment ICC-02/17-138 05-03-2020 ¶ 77 available at https://www.icc-cpi.int/CourtRecords/CR2019_06988.PDF.

military and intelligence officials, was blocked by Trump administration.[206] This reaction raised the problem of sovereignty. Unlike in most civil law systems, the treaties do not dispose any supremacy over U.S. Constitution. Indeed, "[i]n the United States, the court-martial is the oldest system of justice, even pre-dating the Declaration of Independence and the Constitution. During World War II, the number of courts-martial increased dramatically and alleged abuses of individual rights were widespread. This set the stage for major federal law reform, resulting in the passage of the Uniform Code of Military Justice (UCMJ) in 1951".[207] In this respect, it seems that

---

[206] The National Security Advisor, John Bolton declared: "*We will not co-operate with the ICC. We will provide no assistance to the ICC. We will not join the ICC. We will let the ICC die on its own. After all, for all intents and purposes, the ICC is already dead to us*", BBC News, https://www.bbc.com/news/world-us-canada-45474864. (Last visited Apr. 22, 2020). Moreover, it is crucial to emphasize that even a state is not party to Rome statute, the UN Security Council may authorize the prosecution of state concern through a referral proceedings.

[207] *See Forum: Court-Martial, supra* note 143, at 660-661. (Under the UCMJ, any offense committed by a service member on active duty, regardless of location, is triable by court-martial. UCMJ jurisdiction is thus worldwide, on and off duty, on and off base. This approach is markedly different from many other nations, whose jurisdiction does not go beyond their national borders, making prosecutions of alleged overseas wrongdoing significantly more difficult. The UCMJ is a complete set of criminal laws, covering many crimes punishable under civil law (such as murder, rape, assault, and larceny), as well as military offenses that affect good order and discipline (such as dereliction of duty and disobeying a lawful order). U.S. military courts-martial are the preferred forum for LOAC prosecutions of U.S. service members. Article 18 of the UCMJ vests general courts-martial with jurisdiction to try "any person who by the law of war is subject to trial by military tribunal. However, the accused will be charged with the common law crimes under the UCMJ (e.g., several counts of murder), not for war crimes against humanity. Courts-martial are also used for trying enemy prisoners of war for pre-capture LOAC violations or crimes committed during captivity; Article 102 of the Third Geneva Convention mandates that POWs be tried in the same or comparable forum as members of the detaining power's armed forces.

Three types of courts-martial can be convened by a commanding officer: general, special, or summary. The higher the level of court-martial consists of one commissioned officer and may only try enlisted persons for minor offenses with a maximum punishment of one-month confinement. A special court-martial (SPCM) consists of a military judge, defense counsel, prosecutor, and at least three panel members as the jury. A SPCM is for crimes with a maximum punishment of one-year confinement, forfeitures of pay, a reduction in rank, and bad conduct discharge. A general court-martial (GCM) has the same participants as a SPCM but must have at least five panel members as the jury. A GCM's maximum punishment is based upon the maximum allowed by the law for each offense charged, up to and including the possibility (for only the most severe offenses) of death as a punishment. A violation of LOAC involving "grave breaches" would most likely be prosecuted at a GCM and violations of "simple breaches" could potentially be prosecuted at a SPCM.).

the notion of war crimes does not exist in the UCMJ. Additionally, the rights of accused seems to be more protected than those of victims.[208]But, it is not the right place to unpack the UCMJ.

Indeed, key factors upholding the scope of Article 53 determine the interests of justice with regard to victims. So, the consideration of these key factors would be analyzed under the practice of International Criminal Tribunals of Rwanda (ICTR) and for the Former Yugoslavia (ICTY) in favor of the interests of justice. In other words, the International Criminal Tribunals protect the interests of victims in benefit of "interests of justice." The meaning of the "Interests of Justice" under these jurisdictions focuses on the value granted to human dignity after the World War II aftermaths. Further, the Nuremberg Tribunal is, even, the jurisdiction that triggered International Criminal Law. Thus, the objective of the creation of any international criminal jurisdiction after the Nuremberg Trials is to investigate, prosecute or extradite.[209] The gravest international crimes shall never be traded away in consideration of certain key factors mentioned in *infra* in favor of any amnesty in detriment to the interests of victims.

A-Nature Of Crimes With Regard To The Key Factors

With respect to the Human Rights Watch's policy recommendation on the key factors of provisions of Article 53 of ICCSt,[210] the evaluation of Article 53 should focus indispensably on the key factors such as: the gravity of crimes; the age or infirmity of the alleged perpetrator; and the role of the alleged perpetrator,[211]the amount of premeditation and/or planning,[212]the scope and

---

[208] *See* Laurie R. Blank and Gregory P. Noone, *supra* note 158n3, pp. 660-661.
[209] *See*, Michael P. Scharf, *supra* note 42.
[210] *Supra* note 11.
[211] Rome Statute, Art. 53 (2) (c).
[212] *See*, *infra* note 222, Prosecutor v. Krstić.

extent of the crimes,[213]the numbers of victims,[214] the aftermaths of hostilities on the psychology of victims like physical and psychological suffering,[215] and/ or the heinous means or any methods used to commit the crimes.[216]

Regarding the age or infirmity of the alleged perpetrator, the decisions suggest that, at least as to sentencing, the following may be factors to consider: the young age of the accused is indispensable for sentencing[217]as well as the poor health of the accused,[218] and the advanced age of the accused.[219] Additionally, the role of the accused in the commission of crimes, his or her strategy in the commission of crimes,[220] whether he or she directly participated in that commission[221] or is otherwise responsible for the crimes, by having planned, abetted or ordered others to commit them. [222] The informed, voluntary, willing or enthusiastic participation in the

---

[213] *See* Prosecutor v. Plavšić, Case No. IT-00-39, 40/1, ¶ 52 (Int'l Crim. Trib. For the Former Yugoslavia Feb. 27, 2003) (The Trial Chamber held that "The gravity [of offences] is illustrated by: the massive scope and extent of the persecutions; the numbers killed, deported and forcibly expelled; the grossly inhumane treatment of detainees; and the scope of the scope of the wanton destruction of property and religious buildings.").

[214] *Id.*

[215] *Supra* note 160, case No. IT-98-33, ¶ 703([T]he circumstances that the victim detainees were completely at the mercy of their captors, the physical and psychological suffering inflicted upon witnesses to the crime, the indiscriminate, disproportionate, terrifying or heinous means and methods used to commit the crimes [...]).

[216] *Id.*

[217] *See* Prosecutor v. Serushago, Case No. ICTR-98-39 (Trial Chamber), February 5, 1999, ¶¶ 39-42. (The accused young age is considered as mitigating circumstances.).

[218] Prosecutor v. Rutaganda, Case No. ICTR-96-3, ¶¶ 471-73 (Int'l Crim. Trib. For Rwanda r, Dec. 6, 1999). (The Trial Chamber considered Rutaganda's poor health to be a mitigating circumstance).

[219] *Supra* note 210 at¶¶ 95-106. (Here, the deterioration of age of accused may also be considered as a mitigating factor.).

[220]Prosecutor v. Naletilić & Martinović, Case No. IT-98-34, ¶ 744, (Int'l Crim. Trib. For the Former Yugoslavia Sep March 31, 2003). ("[T]he sentence imposed should reflect the relative significance of the role of the accused in the context of the conflict in the former Yugoslavia. However, this has been interpreted to mean that even if the position of an accused in the overall hierarchy in the conflict in the former Yugoslavia was low, it does not follow that a low sentence is to be automatically imposed.").

[221] *See* Prosecutor v. Ruggiu, Case No. ICTR-97-32-I, ¶¶ 53-80(Int'l Crim. Trib. For Rwanda, Jun.1, 2000). (The Trial Chamber considered the following to be mitigating circumstances: the accused's position with *Radio Television Libres des Milles Collines* and in political life [i.e., he was a subordinate at the radio station and played no part in formulating editorial policy] and the fact that he did not personally participate in the killings).

[222] *See* Prosecutor v. Abu Garda, Case No ICC-02/05-02/09, Confirmation of Charges, ¶¶ 71-117 (Feb.8, 2010) (The ICC determined, like the Special Court for Sierra Leone, that peacekeepers are entitled to the protection from attack enjoyed by civilians, except when they directly participate in hostilities. The use of force in self-defense should not lead to a civilian loss in detriment to their protection; Prosecutor v. Krnojelac, Case No. IT-97-25, ¶ 77 (Int'l Crim. Trib. For the Former Yugoslavia, Mar.15, 2002). ("There are, for example, circumstances in which a participant in a joint criminal enterprise will deserve greater punishment than the principal offender deserves. The participant who

crime [223] are absolutely to be considered in the evaluation, like in those tribunals decisions, of Article 53 of the Rome Statute on behalf of the interests of justice.

B-Crucial Additional Factors In Command Responsibility

Examining the question of *mens rea*, the amount of premeditation, or planning[224] and somewhat the numbers of victims.[225] "Command responsibility," sometimes referred to as the Yamashita standard or the Medina standard, and also known as superior responsibility, is the legal doctrine of hierarchical accountability for war crimes.[226] Historically, the concept of "command

---

plans a mass destruction of life, and who orders others to carry out that plan, could well receive a greater sentence than the many functionaries who between them carry out the actual killing.").

[223] *See* Prosecutor v. Rajić, Case No. IT-95-12-S, Review of the Indictment Pursuant to Rule 61 of the Rules of Procedure and Evidence, ¶ 2 (Int'l Crim. Trib. For the Former Yugoslavia Sep. 13, 1996). (Ivica Rajić was accused of ordering the 23 October 1993 attack against the village of Stupni Do, within the Republic of Bosnia-Herzegovina. This attack was allegedly orchestrated by the Crotian Defence Council ("HVO"). Ivica Rajic controlled the armed forced of the self-proclaimed Croatian Community of Herceg-Bosna ("HB"). Rajić is charged [with, among other violations, *wilful* killing, destruction of property, and *deliberate* attack on a civilian population and wanton destruction of a village.]

[224] *Prosecutor v. Krstić*, Case No. IT-98-33 ¶ 711, (Int'l Crim. Trib. For the Former Yugoslavia, Aug. 2, 2001), ("Premeditation may 'constitute an aggravating circumstance when it is particularly flagrant' and motive to some extent [is] a necessary factor in the determination of sentence after guilt has been established.' When a genocide or a war crime, neither of which requires the element of premeditation, are in fact planned in advance, premeditation may constitute an aggravating circumstance. Premediated or enthusiastic participation in a criminal act necessarily reveals a higher level of criminality on the part of the participant. In determining the appropriate sentence, a distinction is to be made between the individuals who allowed themselves to be drawn into a maelstrom of violence, even reluctantly, and those who initiated or aggravated it and thereby more substantially contributed to the overall harm."); *Prosecutor v. Blaškić*, Case No. IT-95-14, ¶ 793 (Trial Chamber, Mar. 3, 2000). ("The premeditation of an accused in a crime tends to aggravate his degree of responsibility in its perpetration and subsequently increases his sentence."); *Prosecutor v. Serushago*, Case No. ICTR-98-39, Sentencing Judgment, ¶¶ 27-30, (Int'l Crim. Trib. For Rwanda, February 5, 1999), (According to the Chamber the fact that the accused "committed the crimes knowingly and with premeditation" constitutes an aggravating circumstances).

[225] *See* Prosecutor v. Semanza, Case No. ICTR-97-20, (Int'l Crim. Trib. For Rwanda May 15, 2003, ¶ 571. (The Trial Chamber considers the number of victims killed by Semanza was an aggravating factor).

[226] *See* Denakpon L. Tchobo, *The Uniform Code of Military Justice (UCMJ) does not expressly affix responsibility to a military leader for violation of the law of war by their subordinates. Are the My Lai Massacre and Abu Ghraib evidence that the U.S. should incorporate command responsibility into its military law? Does the lack of a clear standard in the UCMJ adversely impact discipline within the military, negatively impact senior leaders, or impact the credibility of the U.S.?*, pp. 4-9 (Spring 2019) (unpublished LL.M. note, Case Western Reserve University School of Law) (on file with author).

responsibility" came from the prosecution of General Tomoyuki Yamashita, of the Japanese armed forces in the Philippines. In fact, General Yamashita was tried by the U.S. military commission in Manila, Philippines on the ground of command responsibility *de facto* that he "breached his duty to control the operations of the members of his command by permitting them to commit specified atrocities," adequately alleged a violation of the law of war. General Yamashita appealed to the U.S. Supreme Court on the conviction of the military commission; but, unfortunately for him, the Court denied his motion and upheld the conviction of the commission.[227] Indeed, the military rank and the governmental representations should not constitute an excuse for being shielded from impunity under the international humanitarian law. That is to say that, superiors shall take action to punish crimes committed by their subordinates when they acknowledged of these crimes. Lack of taking action shall be regarded as an aggravating circumstance[228]even as it is a question of abuse of power or official capacity.[229]

Moreover, the subordinate, or soldier in subordination, has the right to deny any illegal order from his or her superior. That is the so-called *intelligent bayonet*[230] in the civil law system. According to that doctrine, the notion of discipline in army or paramilitary cannot constitute an excuse for the soldiers, or subordinates, to obey an illegal order from their superior.[231] Furthermore, the subordinate is aware of his actions.[232] However, the nightmare is to wonder

[227] *In re Yamashita*, 327 U.S. 1, 66 S. Ct. 340 (1946).

[228] *See*, Prosecutor v. Blaškić, *supra* note 207, at ¶ 788. ([A] "command position" is classified "as an aggravating circumstance").

[229] *See* ICC Rules of Procedure and Evidence, ICC-ASP/1/3, Rule 145(2)(b)(ii).

[230] *The " **intelligent bayonet"** theory is in **criminal law** the condemnation of **obedience** to an obviously illegal order. The wording evokes the situation of the soldier (the **bayonet**) who must refuse to carry out an obviously illegal order (because even the military engagement could not make disappear the conscience - the intelligence - of his acts)* available at https://fr.wikipedia.org/wiki/Ba%C3%AFonnette_intelligente. (Accessed on November 3, 2020).

[231] *See* French Penal Code, articles 121-1 and followings.

[232] This raises the question of *mens rea*.

whether this principle would be respected in non-international armed conflicts. The response according to Professor Michael J. Benza[233] is negative.

II-Interpretation Of The Article 53 Under Vienna Convention

The Vienna Convention on the Law of Treaties[234] is an international agreement governing treaties between States. It was drafted by the International Law Commission of the United Nations and adopted on May 23, 1969.[235] The Convention encompasses six parts: the convention helps the States to solve the ambiguities raised in their international agreement. Further it defines first the terms and scope of the agreement; and, second it "lays out the rules for the conclusion and adoption of treaties, including the consent of parties to be bound by treaties and the formulation of reservations that is, declining to be bound by one or more particular provisions of a treaty while accepting the rest."[236] It deals, third, with the application and interpretation of treaties; and fourth, it discusses means of modifying or amending treaties.[237] "The most important part of the convention, Part V, delineates grounds and rules for invalidating, terminating, or suspending treaties and includes a provision granting International Court of Justice jurisdiction in the event of disputes arising from the application of those rules".[238] The final part concerns "the effects on treaties of changes of government within a State, alterations in consular relations between States,

[233] Michael J. Benza is an American Attorney at Law. He teaches U.S criminal law and procedure, death penalty lab, and International Criminal Law at Case Western Reserve University School of Law. (Michael defends the negation of that doctrine in non- international armed conflicts. According to him, anyone in subordination position in non-international armed conflict would not be able to deny his superior order. If he/she does it, he or she may be taken down or killed.). Because his choice is confiscated by the superior.

[234] Vienna Convention was entered into force on January 27, 1980.

[235]Patricia Bauer, article on ,*Vienna Convention on the Law of Treaties*, available at https://www.britannica.com/topic/Vienna-Convention-on-the-Law-of-Treaties. (Accessed on October 4, 2020).

[236] *Id.*

[237] *Id.*

[238] *Id.*

and the outbreak of hostilities between states as well as the rules for depositaries, registration, and ratification".[239] The second and third parts are essential for the aim at our project.

A-Pacta Sunt Servanda, Article 26

Indeed, in light of Article 26, "[e]very treaty in force is binding upon the parties to it and must be performed by them in good faith".[240] This means that State Parties to the Rome Statute have obligation to investigate international crimes commit on their territory and prosecute, or extradite, the alleged perpetrators. Yet, this binding of State Parties does not exclude the States not party. They also have obligation, under the customary international law, *jus cogens*, to prosecute or extradite. Further, in cases of breach of their international obligation, the UN Security Council has the ability to refer, under the Rome Statute, the State concerned to the ICC.[241]

B-Article 27

"A party may not invoke the provisions of its internal law as justification for its failure to perform a treaty."[242] This rule is without prejudice to Article 46.[243] In other words, the domestic law should not prevail over treaties, in cases of prosecution of the gravest international crimes. Amnesties or other form of justice granted to the alleged perpetrators on the ground of peace

---

[239] *Id.*

[240] *See*, Vienna Convention, *supra* note 232, Art. 26*; see* Oliver Dörr, Kirsten Schmalenbach, VIENNA CONVENTION ON THE LAW OF TREATIES, *A Commentary*, Springer, ISBN: 978-3-642-19290-69, pp. 453-473 (2012).

[241] *See* Rome Stature, Art. 13 (b).

[242] *Supra* note 232, Art. 27; also *see*, Oliver Dörr, Kirsten Schmalenbach, *supra* note 239 at 453-473.

[243] Article 46 provides that "[a] State may not invoke the fact that its consent to be bound by a treaty has been expressed in violation of a provision of its internal law regarding competence to conclude treaties as invalidating its consent unless that violation was manifest and concerned a rule of its internal law of fundamental importance".

process in favor the interests of justice are a breach of the law of treaties. Article 53 of Rome Statute of ICC does not contain the word amnesty; further, the Rome Statute does not mention anywhere that the interests of justice means amnesty. However, it is clear in plain language that Article 53 mentions the" interests of victims."[244] Those should not be overlooked or buried under an alibi of peace process without investigation, or prosecution of gross violation of human rights. Furthermore, Article 53 (2) (c) enforces the (1)(c) with the presence of the verb "including," which upholds the interests of victims against any amnesty.[245] This article (2) (c) highlights a negation (is **not**) between the word "prosecution" and the nominal group "the interests of justice." This means first, that the prosecution is indispensable, and second that the terms "interests of justice" does not mean amnesty hidden behind any peace process or negotiation. Therefore, the provisions of Article 53 are clear in light of Article 27 of the Vienna Convention.

C-Article 31

This Article of the Vienna Convention provides that "[a] treaty shall be interpreted in good faith in accordance with the ordinary meaning to be given to the terms of the treaty in their context and in the light of its object and purpose".[246] Here it is, undoubtedly, indisputable that a treaty cannot be effective without its object and purpose. In this regard, the Rome Statute provides:[247]

---

[244] For the purposes of this Statute Art. 53 (1)(c) provides: "Taking into account the gravity of the crime and the ***interests of victims***, there are nonetheless substantial reasons to believe that an investigation would not serve the interests of justice".

[245] "A prosecution is not in the interests of justice, taking into account all the circumstances, **including** the gravity of the crime, ***the interests of victims*** and the age or infirmity of the alleged perpetrator, and his or her role in the alleged crime".

[246] *Supra* note 232, Art. 31; also *see*, Oliver Dörr, Kirsten Schmalenbach, *supra* note 239 at 521-570.

[247] Rome Statute, Preamble.

1. "Affirming that the most serious crimes of concern to the international community as a whole must not go unpunished and that their effective prosecution must be ensured by taking measures at the national level and by enhancing international cooperation," [248]
2. "Determined to put an end to impunity for the perpetrators of these crimes and thus to contribute to the prevention of such crimes,"[249]
3. "Recalling that it is the duty of every State to exercise its criminal jurisdiction over those responsible for international crimes, [...]."[250]

Thus, "the obligation to prosecute" is clearly expressed in the Rome Statute Preamble. Accordingly, "the national courts have the obligation to prosecute" the worst international crimes occur on their territory or extradite the alleged perpetrators before the International Criminal Court. Article 31 of the law of treaties obliges the State Parties to respect their international obligation with regard to the object and purpose of their agreement. In reality, the provisions of Article 53 of the Rome Statute of ICC should not raise any problem. Article 53 is absolutely clear on the concept of the "interests of justice" which requires the prosecution of crimes falling into the jurisdiction of the Court.

---

[248] *Id.* at 4.
[249] *Id.* at 5.
[250] *Id.* at 6.

Conclusion

The prosecutor should have the freedom to exercise his or her discretionary power by initiating an investigation or prosecution for the interests of justice. As a matter of justice, this would be an opportunity to permit the alleged perpetrators to speak out on the reason and the cause of their acts or participation in the commission of crimes. In this respect, victims may also decide to abandon the charge against their perpetrators. By doing so, we argue that amnesty may be granted just in case of mental health, or the age of alleged perpetrators with the aim at attenuating the aggravating circumstance. Finally the presence of the verb *including* in Article 53(2)(c)[251]justifies that Article 53(1)(c) could not be evaluated without Article 53 (2)(c).

[251] This article provides that "[a] prosecution is not in the interests of justice, taking into account all the circumstances, ***including*** the gravity of the crime, the interests of victims and the age or infirmity of the alleged perpetrator, and his or her role in the alleged crime".

Chapter 6: Research Findings

I-Overall Conclusion

The phrase "interests of justice" refers to the "interests of victims" of grave breaches and serious international crimes. These interests should not be traded away for any national peace process. In other words, the notion of peace would be effective if the rule of justice is applied. Accordingly, the meaning of Article 53 of the Rome Statute is the necessity of investigating and prosecuting under the auspices of some requirement factors of criminal law. In other words, there is no justice without victims; whence the obligation to protect the human dignity.

Chapter 1 gave a short literature review on the International Criminal Court, and further presented some of its articles which might constitute a handicap for the effective protection of the interests of victims of the gravest violations of human rights. However, the chapters in infra touched the major question of this thesis, relating to the provisions of Article 53, as well as the gaps of international crimes within the jurisdiction of ICC that are detrimental to the interests of victims.

Furthermore, chapter 2 mentioned that justice should be a process, or action seeking to protect the rights of victims as well as those presumed or accused through a fair trial, for normative goals. The implication of all parties concerned in the process is indispensable for its "double legal character" in benefit of the ethical operationalization of the principle of legality.[252] Otherwise, it would be incomprehensible to highlight the notion of reparation of rights of victims without

[252] Rome Statute, Art. 22.

considering their existence in the triggering of the Court. Left out, in favor of any amnesty might be considered a discrimination to their regard.

For the purpose of this project, chapter 3 outlined the scope of Article 53 of the Rome Statute towards a propulsion of the protection of victims, directly as well as indirectly. Further, it upheld the protection of child soldiers regarded as circumstantial victims because of their age, will and social vulnerability. This status of circumstantial victim should not be an excuse to shield them from impunity; but rather considered as an attenuation in the sentence with regard to the responsibility of their superior, or recruiter. Therefore, the affirmative duty power of the prosecutor should be used for the interests of justice in detriment to any alternative justice methods which do not respond to the real concept of justice. The memory and the vulnerability of victims have to be respected and should not be thrown away in oblivion under the provisions of Article 53 of the Rome Statute for any amnesty because of a misconception of the terms "interests of justice."

Undoubtedly, chapter 4 tackled the core crimes in the Rome Statute of International Criminal Court with their gaps that are in contrast with the respect of human rights. This disadvantages the interests of victims and sometimes may be deleterious to the integrity and fairness of trials under ICC. However, this thesis attempted to wake up the international conscience on the prejudices of those gaps and then proposed a legal framework for the enforcement of the genocide convention under the identification of the new international crime called groupicide. Further, we attempted to draft a proposal of the Convention for its Prevention and Punishment in recommendations.

The prosecutor should have the liberty to exercise his or her discretionary power by initiating an investigation, or prosecution for the interests of justice. As a matter of justice, chapter 5 pointed out the necessity to permit the alleged perpetrators to speak out on the reason and the cause of their acts or participation in the commission of crimes. In this respect, victims may also decide to abandon the charges against their perpetrators. By doing so, we argued that amnesty may be granted just in case of mental health or the age of alleged perpetrators with the aim at attenuating the aggravating circumstance. Because the presence of the verb *including* in Article 53(2)(c)[253]justifies that Article 53(1)(c) could not be evaluated without Article 53 (2)(c).

II-Findings

A-Formula For The Interests Of Justice: Rules Of Investigation (I) And Prosecution (P)

1-Theorem Of The Investigation

RI= [Art. 53(1)(c) + 53 (2) (c)]

NC (Nature of Crime) = LE (Legal Element) = Core Crimes under ICC

Factual Element= Key Factors=FE; RI: Rule of Investigation

RI= NC+FE or ;

RI=LE +FE

RI= [le+fe]

253 This article provides that "[a] prosecution is not in the interests of justice, taking into account all the circumstances, ***including*** the gravity of the crime, the interests of victims and the age or infirmity of the alleged perpetrator, and his or her role in the alleged crime".

RI= (NC)+ (FE) =*lefe*

RI=$(NC) + (FE)$	= [le+fe] =*lefe*

2-Equation of the Prosecution

a. Meaning of symbols

a) CaH: Crimes against Humanity

b) CoG: Crimes of Genocide

c) WC: War Crimes

d) CoA: Crime of Aggression

e) GC: Groupicide

f) P: Presumed criminal or Alleged Perpetrator

g) PR=>: Presumed criminal responsible for

h) [(InCrim)]: Sentence

i) CaH_2^{-11}: Commission of crimes against humanity with eleven counts and two sub-counts

j) WC_{10}^{-5}: Commission of war crimes with five counts and ten sub-counts

k) $[(InCrim)]^{-n}]$: Condemned for *n* years of prison for international crimes

l) $[(WC)]^{-n}$: Convicted of *n* years' imprisonment of war crimes

b. Methods Of Application

This thesis recommends that each count is punished in terms of a ten year of imprisonment. However, I classify child enlistments, torture and rape as sub-counts which shall be severely punished in term of ten years each. This means, for instance, the individuals who rape three women committed three sub-counts, the equivalent of thirty years of imprisonment. But then, in consideration of the principle of double intent, genocide and groupicide, as most heinous crimes, shall directly be punished in term of twenty years under *actus reus*, and ten years for each count. This means that the perpetrator of those crimes automatically receive twenty years sentence. Moreover, in events of war crimes, the amount of child soldiers enlisted would be equal to the same amount of sub-counts. In other words, recruitment of ten child soldiers is the equivalent of ten sub-counts of war crimes. This method may constitute a means of deterrence within the international criminal justice system. The negative sign (less) in this formula depicts *mens rea* in terms of the establishment of the intent of the perpetrator. In the event of that intent would not be determined, particularly in war crimes and crimes against humanity, the person held accountable for superior responsibility will borrow the sentence from the perpetrator. However, the sentence is calculated as following:

- ✓ In war crimes and crimes against humanity: the amount of the counts plus the amount of sub-counts multiplied by ten.
- ✓ In genocide and groupicide: the amount of counts multiplied by ten plus an automatic coefficient of twenty.

B-Hypothesis

Case Study 1

- **War Crimes And Crimes Against Humanity**

The application of theorem of the investigation under the principle of *lefe* finds that Tantapillon committed international crimes such as crimes against humanity and war crimes.

Prosecution charges Tantapillon with two counts of crimes against humanity: murder and forcible transfer (including three sub-counts: torture and rape (two girls)). Prosecution also charges Tantapillon with two counts of war crimes intentionally directed attack against individual civilians, not taking part in hostilities and pillaging. Finally, recruitment of five children transformed in child soldiers as five sub-counts of war crimes.

- **Application**

$$\mathbf{PR}\ [(WC)_5^{-3}] + [(CaH)_3^{-2}] = \mathbf{P} \Rightarrow 80+50 = 130;\ \mathbf{Then,}\ \mathbf{P} \Rightarrow [(InCrim)]^{-130}$$

Hence, Tantapillon is sentenced for one hundred thirty years of imprisonment

$\mathbf{P}[(InCrim)]^{130}]$

Case Study 2

- **Genocide And Groupicide**

The application of theorem of the investigation under the principle of *lefe* finds that Tantapillon committed the most heinous international crimes such as genocide and groupicide. The prosecution charges Tantapillon with two counts of genocide by killing and causing serious bodily, or mental harm on each target group; and one count of groupicidal acts by voting liberticidal law depriving target group to survive socially, culturally, economically and politically.

$$\mathbf{PR}\ [\ (20CoG)^{-2}]\ +\ [\ 20(GC)^{-1}] = \mathbf{P} \Rightarrow 40+30 = 70;\ \mathbf{Then,}\ \mathbf{P} \Rightarrow [(InCrim)]^{-70}$$

Hence, Tantapillon is condemned to seventy years of prison.

$$\mathbf{P}[(\boldsymbol{InCrim})]^{70}]$$

To sum up, each count as well as sub-count is expressed in term of ten years of sentence. This thesis recommends to enhance Articles 77 (1) (a)[254] and 78[255] of the ICCSt by reviewing them in light of this application of the formula of the interest of justice named the rule of IP.

In this regard, Articles 53 (1)(c) and 53 (2)(c) require the application of the rule of IP (the principle of *lefe*) for the interests of justice. This thesis recommends to the Office of the Prosecutor and the Pre-Trial Chambers to use the above formula for determining the interests of justice. In fact, the rule of the investigation would permit to the Office of the Prosecutor to verify whether there are international crimes falling into ICC jurisdiction. If so, the Office of the Prosecutor needs to move forward to the prosecution for the interests of justice. At this stage, the Office of the Prosecutor might apply the second part of the rule of IP which is the equation of the prosecution. Those provisions are the sum of legal elements which are the core crimes within the jurisdiction of the Court and factual elements focusing on the key factors of those articles. The application of

---

[254] The [i]mprisonment for a specific number of year, which may not exceed a maximum of 30 years.

[255] It provides that:

> "1. In determining the sentence, the Court shall, in accordance with the Rules of Procedure and Evidence, take into account such factors as the gravity of the crime and the individual circumstances of the convicted person. 2. In imposing a sentence of imprisonment, the Court shall deduct the time, if any, previously spent in detention in accordance with an order of the Court. The Court may deduct any time otherwise spent in detention in connection with conduct underlying the crime. 3. When a person has been convicted of more than one crime, the Court shall pronounce a sentence for each crime and a joint sentence specifying the total period of imprisonment. This period shall be no less than the highest individual sentence pronounced and shall not exceed 30 years' imprisonment or a sentence of life imprisonment in conformity with article 77, paragraph 1 (b)."

the equation of the prosecution would allow the Office of the Prosecutor to identify the nature of the crime, the number of counts and sub-counts, and then the eventual sentencing that the alleged perpetrator should deserve. Accordingly, the concept of the justice should be regarded under this chart below which depicts its interests.

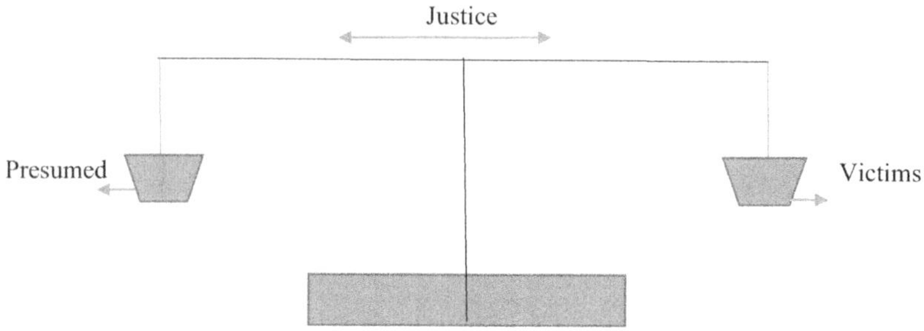

However, the application of Article 53, under the affirmative duty power of prosecutor or pre-trial chambers, might determine the balance of the scale after the application of the rule of IP or after judgement. This position would constitute, the "interests of justice" with regard to the weight of the balance. Thus, the interest of justice would be more objective than the alternative mechanisms focusing on political process.

Moreover, this thesis recommends to the ICC to review and modify the legal definition of the crime of aggression by including the Non-State actors in for the protection of the humanity. Finally, in the aim of enforcing the genocide convention, this thesis recommends the implementation of this proposal for the prevention and the punishment of the groupicide as following:

III-Recommendations

- **Recommendations For Policies Change**

This thesis recommends to the Court the protection of human rights under the provisions of Article 53, which definitely supports the interests of victims. We also recommend, considering amnesty, in last resort, as a principle of attenuating the gravity of crimes **if** the crimes are committed in absence of *mens rea.* In other words, accepting amnesty in case of infirmity, age, mental health. In this perspective, the Court must respect the key factors for the evaluation of Articles 53(1)(c) and 53 (2) (c), such as: age of the alleged perpetrators, nature of crimes, role of alleged perpetrators, their strategies of participation in the commission of crimes, premeditation, and/or planning of alleged perpetrators, their mental health, and victims (including the psychology of survivor's victims and their sufferance above all in events of rape, sexual violence, torture, the respect to the memory of victims died). Any crime that falls within the jurisdiction requires investigation on the first hand; and on the second hand, prosecution based on those key. In plain language, the rule of IP (investigation and prosecution) is equal to legal element (nature of the crime) plus factual elements (key factors set forth above). In this regard, this thesis proposes the implementation of that formula for the balance of the international justice. Additionally, it recommends the adoption of this convention proposal for the enforcement of atrocious crimes.

- **Convention For The Prevention And Punishment Of The Crime Of Groupicide**

Draft proposed for adoption and signature, ratification and accession by General Assembly for its entry into force, in accordance with Article 14.

Preamble

The States Parties to the present Convention,

Considering that, in accordance with the principles proclaimed in the Charter of the United Nations, recognition of the inherent dignity and of the equal and inalienable rights of all members of the human family is the foundation of freedom, justice and peace in the world,

Bearing in mind that the peoples of the United Nations have, in the Charter, reaffirmed their faith in fundamental human rights and in the dignity and worth of the human person, and have determined to protect human being and promote in larger fundamental freedom,

Recognizing that the United Nations has, in the Universal Declaration of Human Rights and in the International Covenants on Human Rights, proclaimed and agreed that everyone is entitled to all the rights and freedoms set forth therein, without distinction of any kind, such as race, colour, sex, language, religion, political or other opinion, national or social origin, property, birth or other status,

Recalling that, in the Universal Declaration of Human Rights, the United Nations has proclaimed that all human beings are born free and equal in dignity and rights. They are endowed with reason and conscience and should act towards one another in a spirit of brotherhood,

Convinced that the human beings living in society, as the fundamental diverse groups of society and the natural environment for the growth and well-being of all their members, should be afforded the necessary protection so that they can fully assume their responsibilities within the community,

Recognizing that all human beings, for the full and harmonious development of his or her personality, should live in peace and security in a family, in group, in environment, in an atmosphere of happiness, love and understanding regardless their opinion, political, association, cultural, religious, affiliation or membership,

Recognizing that persons are targeted, destroyed or deprived of their liberty because of their group affiliation, or membership for decades,

Considering that human beings should feel fully comfortable to live an individual life in society and embody the spirit of the ideals proclaimed in the Charter of the United Nations; and in particular, in the spirit of peace, dignity, tolerance, freedom, equality and solidarity,

Bearing in mind that the need to extend particular protection to the persons living in group according to the nature of their membership or affiliation has been recognized in the Universal Declaration of Human Rights, in the International Covenant on Civil and Political Rights (in particular in Articles 1, 5 and 18), in the International Covenant on Economic, Social and Cultural Rights (in particular in Article 1 and 2) and in the statutes and relevant instruments of specialized agencies and international organizations concerned with the protection of fundamental freedom rights,

Bearing in mind those people need particular protection under the classification of crimes of groupicide.

Convinced that the protection of persons targeted, destroyed, or deprived of their liberty against the nature of their group affiliation, or membership such as: social, cultural, religious, philosophical, and/or political shall be strengthened by the importance of international cooperation,

Hereby agree as hereinafter provided:

Part I

Article 1

State Parties confirm that groupicide, whether committed in time of peace or in time of war, is a crime under international law which they undertake to prevent and to punish.

Article 2

1. For the purposes of the present Convention, a group means a certain reasonable number of people, belonging to a specific community or association sharing a same value, philosophy, or ideology, except the Non-State actors or the members of criminal enterprises, with regard to their socio-cultural, religious, association, political affiliation, or membership.
2. The status of group shall be determined with regard to a reasonable sufficient number, and affiliation, or membership.

Article 3

In the present Convention, groupicide means any of the following acts committed with intent to destroy, in whole or in part, a group of association, social, cultural, religious, philosophical, and/ or such as:

a) Killing members of the group;

b) Causing serious bodily or mental harm to members of the group;

c) Deliberately inflicting on the group conditions of life calculated to bring about its physical destruction in whole or in part;

d) Imposing measures intended to prevent births within the group;

e) Forcibly transferring children of the group to another group;

f) Causing serious prejudice on the group to prevent it from surviving socio-economically;

g) Implementing voting laws in the objective of preventing the members, or group from surviving politically, socially, or economically.

Part II

Article 4

The following acts shall be punishable:

a) Groupicide;

b) Conspiracy to commit groupicide;

c) Direct and public incitement to commit groupicide;

d) Attempt to commit groupicide;

e) Complicity in groupicide.

Article 5

Persons committing groupicide, groupicidal acts, or any of the other acts enumerated in article 4 shall be punished, whether they are constitutionally responsible rulers, public officials or private individuals.

Article 6

1. The State Parties undertake to enact, in accordance with their respective Constitutions, the necessary legislation to give effect to the provisions of the present Convention, and, in particular, to provide effective penalties for persons guilty of groupicide or any of the other acts enumerated in Article 4.

2. State Parties shall take all appropriate measures to ensure that groups are protected against all forms of discrimination or punishment on the basis of their status, activities, expressed opinions, or beliefs of their members.

Article 7

Persons charged with groupicide or any of the other acts enumerated in Article 4 shall be tried by a competent tribunal of the State in the territory of which the act of groupicide was committed, or by such competent international jurisdiction as may have jurisdiction with respect to those State Parties which shall have accepted its jurisdiction.

Article 8

Groupicide and the other acts enumerated in Article 4 shall not be considered as political crimes for the purpose of extradition. The State Parties pledge themselves in such cases to grant extradition in accordance with their laws and treaties in force.

Article 9

Any State Party may call upon the competent organs of the United Nations to take such action under the Charter of the United Nations as they consider appropriate for the prevention and suppression of acts of groupicide or any of the other acts enumerated in Article 4.

Article 10

Disputes between the Contracting Parties relating to the interpretation, application or fulfilment of the present Convention, including those relating to the responsibility of a State for groupicide or for any of the other acts enumerated in Article 4, shall be submitted to the International Court of Justice at the request of any of the parties in dispute.

Part III

Article 11

1. The present Convention shall be open until... for signature on behalf of any Member of the United Nations and of any non-member State to which an invitation to sign has been addressed by the General Assembly.
2. The present Convention shall be ratified, and the instruments of ratification shall be deposited with the Secretary-General of the United Nations.

Article 12

1. One year after its signature, the present Convention may be acceded to on behalf of any Member of the United Nations and of any non-member State which has received an invitation as aforesaid.
2. Instruments of accession shall be deposited with the Secretary-General of the United Nations.

Article 13

Any State Party may at any time, by notification addressed to the Secretary General of the United Nations, extend the application of the present Convention to any or all of the territories for the conduct of whose foreign relations that State Party is responsible.

Article 14

On the day when the first twenty instruments of ratification or accession have been deposited, the Secretary-General shall draw up a procès-verbal and transmit a copy thereof to each Member of the United Nations and to each of the non-member States contemplated in Article 11.

The present Convention shall come into force on the ninetieth day following the date of deposit of the twentieth instrument of ratification or accession.

Any ratification or accession effected subsequent to the latter date shall become effective on the ninetieth day following the deposit of the instrument of ratification or accession.

Article 15

A State Party may denounce the present Convention by written notification to the Secretary-General of the United Nations. Denunciation becomes effective one year after the date of receipt of the notification by the Secretary-General.

Article 16

1. Any State Party may propose an amendment and file it with the Secretary-General of the United Nations. The Secretary-General shall thereupon communicate the

proposed amendment to State Parties, with a request that they indicate whether they favor a conference of State Parties for the purpose of considering and voting upon the proposals. In the event that, within four months from the date of such communication, at least one third of the State Parties favor such a conference, the Secretary-General shall convene the conference under the auspices of the United Nations. Any amendment adopted by a majority of States Parties present and voting at the conference shall be submitted to the General Assembly for approval.

2. An amendment adopted in accordance with paragraph 1 of the present article shall enter into force when it has been approved by the General Assembly of the United Nations and accepted by a two thirds majority of State Parties.
3. When an amendment enters into force, it shall be binding on those State Parties which have accepted it, other State Parties still being bound by the provisions of the present Convention and any earlier amendments which they have accepted.

Article 17

The Secretary-General of the United Nations is designated as the depositary of the present Convention.

Article 18

The Secretary-General of the United Nations shall notify all Members of the United Nations and the non-member States contemplated in article XI of the following:

(a) Signatures, ratifications and accessions received in accordance with article 12;

(b) Notifications received in accordance with Article 13;

(c) The date upon which the present Convention comes into force in accordance with article 14;

(d) Denunciations received in accordance with Article 15;

(e) The abrogation of the Convention in accordance with article 16;

Article 19

1. The present Convention shall be registered by the Secretary-General of the United Nations on the date of its coming into force.
2. The original of the present Convention shall be deposited in the archives of the United Nations.
3. A certified copy of the Convention shall be transmitted to each member of the United Nations and to each of the non-member States mentioned in Article 12.

Article 20

The original of the present Convention, of which the Arabic, Chinese, English, French, Russian and Spanish texts are equally authentic, shall be deposited with the Secretary-General of the United Nations. IN WITNESS THEREOF the undersigned plenipotentiaries, being duly authorized thereto by their respective governments, have signed the present Convention.

- **Recommendation for Future Research**

Creating a software based on the "rules of IP" that permits the Office of the Prosecutor (OTP) to easily assess and identify the crimes falling into her/his jurisdiction. After investigation, the OTP needs to insert all the evidence in the software. So the software will evaluate at first stage the facts and verify whether there are international crimes committed within ICC jurisdiction. If so, the software will show up under the equation of the prosecution the nature of crimes committed, the number of counts and sub-counts, and then the eventual sentence the alleged perpetrator should deserve.

Bibliography

Textbooks And Articles

Laurie R. Blank and Gregory P. Noone, INTERNATIONAL LAW AND ARMED CONFLICT, *Fundamental Principles and contemporary Challenges in the Law of War*, pp. 714-715 (2013)

Christine Evans, THE RIGHT TO REPARATION IN INTERNATIONAL LAW FOR VICTIMS OF ARMED CONFLICT, Cambridge University, p. 102 (2012)

William Schabas, *An introduction to the International Criminal Court* ,4th, CUP England, pp. 64-66 (2011)

K.M. Clarke, Fictions of Justice: The ICC and the Challenge of Legal Pluralism in Sub-Saharan Africa, Cambridge University Press, pp. 20-23 (2009)

William A. Schabas and Ramesh Thakur, ATROCITIES AND INTERNATIONAL ACCOUNTABILITY: *Beyond Transitional Justice*, United Nations University Press, pp.143-145 (2007)

Jean-Marie Henckaerts & Louise Doswald-Beck, 1 CUSTOMARY INTERNATIONAL HUMANITARIAN LAW, 569-570 (2005)

Oliver Dörr, Kirsten Schmalenbach, VIENNA CONVENTION ON THE LAW OF TREATIES, *A Commentary*, Springer, ISBN: 978-3-642-19290-69, pp. 453-473 (2012)

S. Kendall and S. Nouwen, Representational Practices at the International Criminal Court: *The Gap Between Juridified and Abstract Victimhood*, 76 Law and Contemporary Problems, 235-262, at 258 (2014)

R. Killean and L. Moffett, *Victim Legal Representation before the ICC and* ECCC, 15 JICJ, pp.713-740 (2017).

Michael Scharf, "*The Amnesty exception to the Jurisdiction of the International Criminal Court*," Cornell International Law Journal, vol. 32 (1999), 507, 521-22.

Michael P. Scharf, "An Essay on Trading Justice for Peace", 63 Washington and Lee Law Review 339-376, (2006).

Michael P. Scharf, *The Letter of the Law: The Scope of the International Legal Obligation to Prosecute Human Rights Crimes*, 59 LAw & CoNTEMP. PROBS. n1, (1996).

Michael P. Scharf, *How the War Against ISIS Changed International Law*, 48 Case W. Res. J. Int'l L. p 14. (2016).

Mahnoush H. Arsanjani, "*The Rome Statute of the International Criminal Court*," American Journal of International Law, vol. 22 (1999), p. 38.

Katherine G. Southwick, *Srebrenica as Genocide? The Krstić Decision and the Language of the Unspeakable*, YALE HUMAN RIGHTS & DEVELOPMENT L.J. 08, at *227 (2005).

Giuliano Turone, "*Powers and Duties of the Prosecutor*, "*in The Rome Statute of the International Criminal Court: A Commentary*, edited by Antonio Cassese, Paola Gaeta & John R.W.D. Jones (Oxford: oxford University press, 2002), P. 1142

Talita De Souza Dias, International Criminal Court and Tribunals, "Interests of Justice *": Defining the scope of Prosecutorial Discretion in Article 53 (1) (c) and 53 (2) (c) of the Rome Statute of International Criminal Court,* Leiden Journal of International Law, vol. 30, pp. 731-751.

Kate Allan," Prosecution and Peace: *A Role for Amnesty Before the ICC?"*, 39 Denv.J. Int'l L. & Pol'y 239 (2019).

Kristin Henrard, The Viability of National Amnesties in View of the Increasing Recognition of Individual Criminal Responsibility at International Law, 8 *MSU-DCL J. Int'l L*. 595, 646 (1999).

Denakpon L Tchobo, Tension between Peace and Justice under ICC: *Influence of Alternative Justice Mechanisms*, LLM note, pp. 26-28. (2019).

Denakpon L. Tchobo, *The Uniform Code of Military Justice (UCMJ) does not expressly affix responsibility to a military leader for violation of the law of war by their subordinates. Are the My Lai Massacre and Abu Ghraib evidence that the U.S. should incorporate command responsibility into its military law? Does the lack of a clear standard in the UCMJ adversely impact discipline within the military, negatively impact senior leaders, or impact the credibility of the U.S.?*, pp. 4-9 (Spring 2019) (unpublished LL.M. note, Case Western Reserve University School of Law) (on file with author).

Human Rights Watch (HRW), *The Meaning of ''the Interests of Justice'' In article 53 of the Rome Statute*, Policy Paper, (June 2005) at p. 12;

Diane Orentlicher, "Settling Accounts: *The Duty to Prosecute Human Rights Violations of a Prior Regime* ", (1991) 100 Yale Law Journal 2537.

Amnesty International, "Open Letter to the Chief Prosecutor of the International Criminal Court: Comments on the Concept of the Interests of justice", drafted by Martin Macpherson, senior director of the International Law and Organizations Program, 17 June 2005.

Bassiouni, *International Law and the Holocaust*, 9 CAL. W. INT'L L.J. 202 (1979).

Kleffner, *The Impact of Complementarity on National Implementation of Substance International Criminal Law,* 1 Journal of International Criminal Justice, p 86 (2003).

John Dugard, *Possible Conflicts of Jurisdiction with Truth Commissions*, *in The Statute de Rome*: Of The International Criminal Court: A commentary 700 (Antonio Cassese et al, ed., 2002).

Carsten Stahn, *Complementarity, Amnesties and Alternative Forms of Justice*, 3 J. Int'l L Crim. Just. 695, 708, pp 711- 716 (2005).

John B. Bellinger III and Vijay M. Padmanabhan, Detention Operations In Contemporary Conflicts*: Four Challenges For The Geneva Conventions And Other Existing Law*, 105 A.J.I.L. 201, 201, at *204 (2011)

Arthur H. Garrison," Defining the Meaning and Purpose of Justice, Law, and Criminal Justice*: A Hermeneutical Judeo-Christian Biblical Perspective*", 55 J. Cath. Leg. Stud. 1 at * 5. (2016).

John Jacques Rousseau, *The Social Contract* or *Principles of Political Rights*, (1976).

Farooq Hassan, *The Theoretical Basis of Punishment in International Criminal Law,* 15 Case W. Res. J. Int'l L. 39, p 50. (1983)

Stone, *Hopes and Loopholes in the 1974 Definition of Aggression*, 71 AM. J. Int'l L. 224 (1977)

B. FERENCZ, *2 Defrn4ng International Aggression: The Search For World Peace,* 50- 53 (1975)

Andreas O'Shea, AMNESTY FOR CRIME IN INTERNATIONAL LAW AND PRACTICE, Kluwer International Law, p. 317 (2002)

Elizabeth B. Ludwin King, *AMNESTIES IN A OF TIME OF TRANSITION*, 41 Geo. Wash. Int'l L. Rev. 577, at** 617-618 (2010)

M. Macpherson, *Comments on the concept of the interests of justice*, Amnesty International, Open Letter to the Chief Prosecutor of the International Criminal Court, Jun. 17 (2005)

Roos Haer, *Children and armed conflict: looking at the future and learning from the past*, Third World Quarterly, 40:1, 74-91

Jo Becker declaration, *Record Number of Countries on US Child Soldiers Blacklist*, ¶ 2 June 29, 2020

C. Gallavin, *Article 53 of The Rome Statute of The International Criminal Court: In the Interests of Justice?,* 14 King's College Law Journal 179, at 193–197 (2003)

Yvonne MCDermott, *Victims And International Law: Remedies In The Courtroom*, Hague Justice Journal, 4 No. 3, P 199 (2009)

Ivana Nizich, *International Law Weekend Proceedings: International Tribunals and Their Ability to Provide Adequate Justice: Lessons from The Yugoslav Tribunal*, 7 ILSA J Int'l & Comp L 353, at *354-*358 (2001)

Telford Taylor, *Final Report to the Secretary of the Army on the Nuremberg War Crimes Trials under control Council Law*, No. 10 64-65 (1949)

Leila Nadya Sadat *Putting Peacetime First: Crimes Against Humanity And The Civilian Population Requirement*, 31 Emory Int'l L. Rev. 197, at *217 (2017)

John B. Bellinger III and Vijay M. Padmanabhan, Detention Operations In Contemporary Conflicts*: Four Challenges For The Geneva Conventions And Other Existing Law*, 105 A.J.I.L. 201, 201, at *204 (2011)

David A. Elder, *The Historical Background of Common Article 3 of the Geneva Convention of 1949*, 11 Case W. Res. J. Int'l L. 37 (1979)

Dapo Akande & Antonios Tzanakopoulos, *The Crime of Aggression in the ICC and State Responsibility*, 58, Harvard J. Int'l L. 32, Spring (2017)

MacKennan Graziano and Lan Mei, 58, *The Crime of Aggression under the Rome Statute and Implications for Corporate Accountability*, 58 Harvard J. Int'l L. 60, Spring (2017).

Antonio Cassese, *The Nicaragua and Tadić Tests Revisited in Light of the ICJ Judgment on Genocide in Bosnia*, 18 Eur. J. Int'l. L. 649, 651–667 (2007)

Charles Doyle, *Statute of Limitation in Federal Criminal Cases*, CRS Report RS21121, n18, p 2, Nov. 14 (2017)

WEBSITES

https://www.ohchr.org.

https://www.how-the-icc-works.aba-icc.org/cases/2011-unsc-resolution-on-libya-referral/

http:// www.icc-cpi-cpi.int/press/pressreleases.html

https://www.merriam-webster.com/dictionary/amnesty

https://www.fas.org/sgp/crs/misc/RL31253.pdf.

https://www.un.org/en/genocideprevention/documents/atrocity-crimes/Doc.27_convention%20statutory%20limitations%20warcrimes.pdf

www.redress.org.

https://www.research.un.org/en/docs/ga/quick/regular/26 (Accessed on September 22, 2020).

https://www.un.org/en/genocideprevention/documents/atrocitycrimes/Doc.28_Principles%20of%20international%20cooperation%20in%20detection.pdf

https://www.lawinsider.com/dictionary.

https://www.tandfonline.com/doi/full/ DOI: 10.1080/01436597.2018.1552131

https://www.hrw.org/topic/childrens-rights/child-soldiers

https://www.hrw.org/news/2020/06/29/record-number-countries-us-child-soldier-blacklist

http://wwww.icc-cpi.int/Menus/ASP/states+parties

https://treaties.un.org/doc/publication/unts/volume%2078/volume-78-i-1021-english.pdf.

https://www.treaties.un.org/doc/publication/ctc/uncharter.pdf

http://www.adh-geneve.ch/RULAC/pdf/Common-Article-3.pdf

http://www. crc.org/en/doc/assets/files/publications/icrc-002-0173.pdf

http://www.ejil.org/pdfs/18/4/233.pdf

https://www.bbc.com/news/world-us-canada-45474864

https://fr.wikipedia.org/wiki/Ba%C3%AFonnette_intelligente

https://www.britannica.com/topic/Vienna-Convention-on-the-Law-of-Treaties

Reports And Resolutions

International Criminal Court, Report of the Court on the Strategy in Relation to Victims, 10 November 2009, ICC-ASP/8/45, ¶ 6

Inter-Am. Comm'n H.R., Report No. 26/92, OEA/Ser.L./V/II.83, doc. 14, corr. 1 (1992-93) [hereinafter El Salvador Case];

Inter-Am. Comm'n H.R., Report No. 28/92, OEA/Ser.L./ V/II.83, doc. 14, corr. 1 (1993);

Inter-Am. Comm'n H.R., Report No. 29/92, OEA/Ser.L./V/II.83, doc. 14, corr. 1 (1993)

Paper for the 8th Assembly of States Parties, The Hague, 18–26 November 2009

ICC Rules of Procedure and Evidence, Adopted by the Assembly of States Parties, New York, 3–10 September 2002, Official Records ICC-ASP/1/3.

Article 1, UN Declaration of Basic Principles of Justice for Victims of Crime and Abuse of Power, adopted by UN General Assembly Resolution 40/34 of 29 November 1985

U.N. Human Rights Comm., Compilation of General Comments and General Recommendations Adopted by Human Rights Treaty Bodies, cmt. 20, P 15, U.N. Doc. HRI/GEN/1/Rev.1 (July 29, 1994).

G.A. Res. 2840 (XXVI), P 4, U.N. Doc A/8429 Dec.18, (1971)

G.A. Res. 3074 (XXVIII), P 1, U.N. Doc A/9030 Dec. 3, p5 (1973)

Universal Declaration of Human Rights, Adopted 10 December 1948, GA Res. 217 A (III)

International Covenant on Civil and Political Rights (ICCPR), adopted 16 December 1966, GA Res. 2200A (XXI), 999 UNTS 171

International Covenant on Economic, Social and Cultural Rights (CESCR), adopted 16 December 1966, GA Res. 2200A (XXI), UN Doc. A/6316 (1966), 993 UNTS 3

Convention for the Protection of Human Rights and Fundamental Freedoms (ECHR), adopted 4 November 1950, ETS 5, 213 UNTS 221; International Convention on the Elimination of All Forms of Racial Discrimination (CERD), adopted 21 December 1965, GA Res. 2106 (XX), annex, UN Doc. A/6014 (1966), 660 UNTS 195

American Convention on Human Rights (ACHR), adopted 22 November 1969, OAS Treaty Ser. No. 36, 1144 UNTS 123

African Charter on Human and Peoples' Rights (AChHR), adopted 27 June 1981, OAU Doc. CAB/LEG/67/3 rev. 5, 1520 UNTS 217

Van Boven/ Bassiouni Principles, << Basic Principles and Guidelines on the Right to a Remedy and reparation for Victims of Gross violations of International Human Rights Law and serious violations of International humanitarian law>>, adopted by the Commission on Human Rights in its resolution 2005/35 of 19 April 2005 and by the Economic and Social Council in its resolution 2005/30 of 25 July 2005 in which the Council recommended to the UN General Assembly that also adopted it and proclaimed in its resolution 60/147 of 16 December 2005.

Convention on the Prohibition of the Development Production and Stockpiling of Bacteriological (Biological) and Toxic Weapons and on their Destruction, 27 U.N. G.A.O.R. Supp. (No. 30) at 17, U.N. Doc. A/8189 (1970);

Geneva Protocol for the Prohibition of the Use in War of Asphyxiating, Poisonous or Other Gases of Bacteriological Methods of Warfare, Doc. C. 362 M. 135 1927 IX (1927)

Treaty Banning Nuclear Weapon Tests in the Atmosphere, in Outer Space and Under Water, Aug. 5, 1963, 14 U.S.T. 1313, T.I.A.S. No. 5433

Treaty on the Prohibition of The Emplacement of Nuclear Weapons on the Sea Bed and The Ocean Floor and in the Sub-Soil Thereof, 25 U.N. G.A.O.R. Supp. (No. 28) at 11, U.N. Doc. A/8189 (1970)

Treaty on Principles Governing the Activities of States in Exploration and Use of Outer Space, Including the Moon and Other Celestial Bodies, Jan. 27, 1967, 18 U.S.T. 2410, T.I.A.S. No. 6347

Antarctic Treaty, Dec. 1, 1959, 12 U.S.T. 794, T.I, S. No. 4780

Publisher: Eliva Press Global Ltd

Email: info@elivapress.com

Made in the USA
Las Vegas, NV
30 March 2026

44475362R00075